Dating

Practical Advice From a Female Dating Coach
(A Dating Coach's Step-by-step Guide to Finding Love at Any Age)

Seymour Pricers

Published By **Elena Holly**

Seymour Pricers

All Rights Reserved

Dating: Practical Advice From a Female Dating Coach (A Dating Coach's Step-by-step Guide to Finding Love at Any Age)

ISBN 978-1-77485-476-1

No part of this guidebook shall be reproduced in any form without permission in writing from the publisher except in the case of brief quotations embodied in critical articles or reviews.

Legal & Disclaimer

The information contained in this ebook is not designed to replace or take the place of any form of medicine or professional medical advice. The information in this ebook has been provided for educational & entertainment purposes only.

The information contained in this book has been compiled from sources deemed reliable, and it is accurate to the best of the Author's knowledge; however, the Author cannot guarantee its accuracy and validity and cannot be held liable for any errors or omissions. Changes are periodically made to this book. You must consult your doctor or get professional medical advice before using any of the suggested remedies, techniques, or information in this book.

Upon using the information contained in this book, you agree to hold harmless the Author from and against any damages, costs, and expenses, including any legal fees potentially resulting from the application of any of the information provided by this guide. This disclaimer applies to any damages or injury caused by the use and application, whether directly or indirectly, of any advice or information presented, whether for breach of contract, tort, negligence, personal injury, criminal intent, or under any other cause of action.

You agree to accept all risks of using the information presented inside this book. You need to consult a professional medical practitioner in order to ensure you are both able and healthy enough to participate in this program.

TABLE OF CONTENTS

Introduction 1

Chapter 1: The Reasons Women Get Used To Terrible Dates 5

Chapter 2: Folks This Is The Way To Begin To Approach Women You're Interested In 14

Chapter 3: Tips For Dating For Men 19

Chapter 4: Discover Masculine Traits 31

Chapter 5: Factors You Should Be Educated About 38

Chapter 6: Law Of Attraction And Dating 43

Chapter 7: Confidence Vs Arrogance 52

Chapter 8: How To Say And Not Say 63

Chapter 9: Becoming Your Strongest And Best Self 81

Chapter 10: What Should I Do The Next Date? 97

Chapter 11: Learning To Play The Game 102

Chapter 12: Volume Dating Like A Winner 108

Chapter 13: Making The First Impression And Ensuring It's The Last 118

Chapter 14: Language Of Flirting: 25 Phrases Women Love 129

Chapter 15: More Information About Dating 140

Chapter 16: "Finish Strong" 144

Chapter 17: The Hints Are For Riddles. 148

Chapter 18: Read Through Women's Profiles................... 156

Chapter 19: How To Keep Her Attracted To You, Or How To Have A Long-Term Relationship.. 166

Chapter 20: What Makes A Perfect Date Work So Well ... 175

Conclusion 182

Introduction

Everyone would like to be loved. Although it might sound cliché but love is a powerful force that can move mountains and improve all aspects of your life. It enhances your mental and emotional health as well as your physical health and overall satisfaction. It lets us feel different emotions and emotions which makes us feel like as a normal human being. It causes you to think about the positive things that happen in your life , even the negatives. It can ward off negative thoughts because love is the only thing that can be defeated in the first place, surely? It keeps you conscious and physically active since you are fit for love. The most important thing is that the feeling of love is a source of happiness because it is so strong, it could transform your life in a flash. Who doesn't like to awake every day with pure joy and love? Everyone no matter how horrible or lonely is, always wants to find someone who can be able to share the joys and lows of the day. No matter what age, whether old or young being with a person in your day-to-day life makes it more worthwhile living. That's why they say "no human being is an isle."

For majority of us, finding the perfect person to discuss all of these experiences with is an exhausting task. it can be it's a long and difficult one. It's like a daunting task with all our expectations and standards. We begin to think about the end of things when we have just begun and that, my dear is when everything goes down. There is no one who knows the best method to find that "right" solution. You'll have to discover for yourselfat some time or an additional point.

But, don't despair and feel negative about it. That's the sole reason that the term "dating" was created. It allowed everyone from all kinds of backgrounds to discover and meet that special person they would like to live the remainder of their lives and not. Based on your goals it is an excellent way to find an ideal partner for yourself. With the advances in our world that we have today making dating simpler for everyone.

This book can guide you through everything you should be aware of about dating. From finding the perfect person to meet to the planning you have to make for getting yourself prepared and knowing what to say and to avoid saying as well as being aware of what you should do in the event that you have a problem and finishing well to ensure you get the chance to meet again.

Another advantage of this book is that it offers you examples of what you must and should not to say when you are dating. Beginning a good and meaningful conversation has a significant impact in a relationship because it will determine the flow of your evening. Most people are in a relationship because they want to meet the person they are dating. They may also be interested in determining if what they're looking for in a person can be found in your. This book will certainly aid you in saying the right things and avoid the subjects that you need to stay clear of.

Don't be scared to make mistakes. This book is about teaching you and helping you prior to, during as well after the date. But, you cannot do all these things as they're too numerous to keep in mind. Take your lessons from mistakes, and be certain to follow the guidelines to make your date a success.

Chapter 1: The Reasons Women Get Used To Terrible Dates

Are you interested in knowing the reason women go on bad dates? The reason is that most guys are unsure of what makes a good first date.

It's an impressive way to begin a novel however I'm not the type of man who beats around with the subject. I'll give you the straight facts right from the beginning until the end. No matter if you enjoy the way I dress or not I'm aware of the number of men I've helped and I'm sure of what I'm about give you. So, let's begin right now.

What is it that makes men so unaware of what makes the ideal kind of date is?

Simply put, the majority of men are naive about the ideal date because they are trying too to hard. If you've ever had the pleasure of taking an acquaintance on dates, I'm pretty sure you've had to deal with at some of the issues I'm about to discuss.

Three major blunders that men make when they are dating:

#1 - The majority of men will go on a date they believe they'll like.

#2 - The majority of men want to shell out a large amount of money to impress women.

#3 - The majority of men do not behave like they would when they are dating.

But you're far from "most guys," and by the time you've done reading this book, you'll know how to be the man you want to be.

Do you want to know the one connection in the three mistakes? These are all deceitful.

Involuntary or purposeful Each of these errors will fool the woman into thinking that you're someone else you're not. There are a lot of issues with fooling women and we'll take an in-depth look at the various mistakes to make sure you don't fall for them.

#1 - The majority of men will go on a date they think they'll like.

You may be thinking "Isn't exactly the thing I'm supposed to perform?" The answer is non-sensical, in fact, not at all.

The issue when you take a woman out on a date you believe she'll like is that it fools her into thinking that you're also happy with the location and the things you're doing. This is a recipe to fail in the future. I've seen this a thousand times. Man takes his wife to the movies to see a romantic comedy because he is not a fan of romantic comedy. A man also goes bowling with a woman when they're not going to an arcade by himself. A different man goes with his wife to a fancy restaurant after eating quick food, or order takeaway every other evening.

The reason for this to be an act of deceit because, if these are the actions you take the first time you go on with her the woman you're considering dating believes that this will be something you like doing. They will always be remembered as the first dates. They'll be in her memory. She'll share with her acquaintances about them. She'll inform her family members about the dates. Anyone she has a close relationship with will know about these first dates. And you'll end up into a box is impossible to leave without much difficulty.

For instance: You go bowling with a lady because she once mentioned it and you believe she'd like it. She informs her family members, friends and her mom that you have taken her bowling. They all comment,

"That's so perfect, you're addicted to bowling! It's something you will do often!"

It's just not something you'd want to be doing often. It's even not something you'd like to do in the first place. You went to her in the hopes that she'd enjoy it, and consequently prefer you to her. However, in reality, she doesn't love you more. She is only interested in what you tricked her into believing about her. How difficult do you think it will be to inform her how much you dislike bowling?

Then we'll look at what you can do in the future. However, first we'll talk about error number two.

#2 - The majority of men try to shell out a significant amount of money to impress women.

It's not the right thing to do. It not only deceives her into thinking that the amount you pay for this initial date will be normal however, a lot of women are able to see at this.

You can choose to be with a woman who is able to recognize the lie or you'll to meet a woman who is as ignorant as you. They'll fall for the deceit and imagine the luxuries dates you'll be on and then discover that the first date was not even who you are. It doesn't matter if it was intentional or not it is a common tactic to bait and switch.

I receive questions frequently regarding how a first date will go. We'll discuss that later. It's best to begin by defining what you should not do. Don't invite a woman to a costly dinner or a movie in which you purchase all the things she needs, then conclude the date by bringing her a dessert from her favourite restaurant that is miles away. If you don't are able and willing to do this throughout your life.

As with the previous mistake it is a deliberate act of deceit due to the way you're showing yourself to be. You're creating a visual of yourself from the very first date that you go on with a woman and they'll be able to be able to remember them clearly. Everyone you know will be able to hear about the amount of money you put into her, and be thrilled to learn that she met an individual who will delight her for the remainder all of the time.

The truth is, you don't have that amount of money and would be unable to be able to keep up with the way these first couple of date nights were spent. You're deceiving her to believe that it's a fairytale. What happens when you sabotage her desires with a complete change in the amount that you invest in dates? When will you're out of money? Are you going to have a conversation about the fact that you aren't able to spend this much? What will you tell her that the first date weren't clear of who you are?

This is the issue when it comes to simple deceit during the initial stages of dating an individual. You can call it what you like bait and switch exaggerating yourself, over-promising and underdelivering. It is only perceived as the same thing: Deception.

#3 - The majority of men aren't themselves when they're with a woman.

Third mistake is an important role in the two previous mistakes. Men don't always behave as if they're meeting women. Going to places with her because you think she'll be interested in the place and spending more than you would for a longer period are two of the main reasons for not acting as you do. However, there are other types of acting out as you do aside from these mistakes.

As I've begun to date women, I've observed my friends behave completely differently than what they typically do. They speak in a different way. They wear different clothes. They behave differently. They present an untrue persona, and they make people believe that they are who they aren't. This is the most deceiving kind of deceit because you're not just fooling women into believing that you know the amount of money you spend or where you prefer to go. It goes further by giving women an entirely false impression of who you truly are as an individual.

If you find that a woman brings out your best qualities and makes you the confident person you've always wanted to be, then that's one thing. However, if you're actively changing your character solely because you think she'll be more interested in you I believe that your friend is a lie. The house you are building is that is made of glass. Once you start to reveal your true self the walls will begin to break. It will not take long for the glass home to crack into small, sharp shards.

Consider the situation as follows: The way you behave in the initial phases of dating is what women consider to be truthful. Your words and how you conduct yourself is the picture you create for her. If she is truly happy with the persona you constructed, you'll need to continue to be that way throughout the duration period of your friendship. In the end this will be impossible. You're basically telling her what you really are. Wouldn't it be better to be more as you do?

Avoid these mistakes

A lot of people make these errors. Now that you are aware of these mistakes, you must be sure you do not make them again. Be who you are. If you find that a girl doesn't appreciate the person you are as a whole You shouldn't take it as a reason to be disappointed. Instead, take it as a sign the relationship was not meant to be, and probably wouldn't last in the first place.

Be yourself. Being yourself can make dating easy in the beginning since there is no need to engage in any deceitful acts to maintain the relationship. The perfect woman is likely to come along who appreciates the person you are, that's why you don't have to maintain a fake persona. You'll only need to be the person you really are.

Chapter 2: Folks This Is The Way To Begin To Approach Women You're Interested In

1. Don't comment about her appearance.

"As far as I can be concerned, commenting on your body appearances is an undesirable thing to do. It's like saying, 'hello I've been scrutinizing your body and decided I'm going to make you feel guilty and I'm going to continue to inquire about you until you agree to let me in'. Finding out information or saying something regarding something happening in the environment is the most effective choice.'

2. Chat casually.

"Attempt to get them to talk about something that is commonplace, look at the book they're reading or the film/game that's on their shirt and even the weather. If, for any reason, you are on the occasion that they do not respond or seem to be interested Don't repeat yourself your request, but don't get too annoyed with them, especially when they don't respond or are acting like that in a "I'm feeling awkward and off-kilter' not causing too much bother and you're not too worried, go away.'

3. Peruse her non-verbal communication.

If she doesn't appear at all interested (begins to walk away, makes short comments) relax and allow her to be. It seems to me that this is the point where a lot of men fail, not going further and not allowing the lady enough room.'

4. Choose your settings carefully.

For me, it's more related to the situation when you shouldn't be able to approach me. In a vehicle that is open, with headphones on, or when I'm not in a state of mind do not approach. I'm not the type of person to engage in conversation. If I'm just browsing in an eatery or shop or just a friendly greeting, "hello, I've seen you and you seem to be an attractive person to talk to or anything that isn't associated with my appearance in that case I'll probably be in!

I've had people visit me in coffeehouses when I'm reading or trying to inquire about what I'm doing. If I have to think about it, I'll tell them easily, and in most situations I'm okay by joking and ranting about my certificate. Bring me something academic.'

5. Take a step back from the arrogance.

"Certainty" is not egotism. Learn to recognize the phrase that haughtiness is among the most offensive thing that exists for me. Indeed, I welcome any conversation, and I'm not going to be able to accept that you're a slither on the off chance you rely on me, and then talk as if you're in agreement.

I can tell if you're nervous and I'm not going to make a judgment on you because of it. If you're not making random comments regarding my appearance, or offering an unflattering line to me, we must enjoy a pleasant conversation.'

6. Smile at her.

"I believe that humor is amazing for ice-breaking or intriguing questions. If they're not enthralled by the topic, they're likely exhausted to speak with at any time.'

7. Notice your environmental factors.

"The best method is to express a impression about something that's happening inside the area. There's a good chance she'll have an opinion on it or won't be looking into it more.'

8. Take note of the sisterhood.

Don't try to praise any woman by putting another lady down. For example, you shouldn't say things like "awesome You're so much smarter than other young ladies' as it is a massive warning.

9. Do not praise her appearance, but her body.

If you start with a praise ensure that it is authentic and not about something she was introduced to the world by.

"I am always greeted with the comment 'your eyes are beautiful" and feel so odd and don't know what to say. Once I said "hello, much appreciated and I received them for the day of my birthday'.

10. Think about what makes her different.

"I'm curious to know why you're interested in having a conversation with this beautiful lady regardless. Assuming that your primary answer is that she's beautiful Move on it is likely that you're one of five people within close proximity who think so also. Assuming she's a style of hers or a book she's sifting through or something that's more than just being attractive, begin with this.'

11. Don't over-think it.

Try not to talk to them as if they're teenagers or converse with them as they're real people.'

Chapter 3: Tips For Dating For Men

Perhaps the most unfortunate outcome of trying to meet one of your male friends could be fearing appearing as creepy. It's the main reason behind why many males from feeling relaxed or comfortable when they meet women they consider attractive. Many men are aware that women can have a higher degree of sensitivity than males usually, in all instances, when it comes to their partners in love or sexual relationships. This naturally adds pressure to make yourself stand out in a positive way yet not appear depressed or even pathetic in the same breath. This is one of the main reasons that men prefer to stay clear of women. The majority of men believe that it is best to stay clear of rejection and think it's better to think they're unattainable? It isn't easy to find a middle way. How do you find a equilibrium?

It's an unlucky situation for those who are introverted or shy. There are probably every possible scenario that could occur when you meet a beautiful woman. But being stressed out contemplating any error you could make can take you to a fantasy world built on anxiety. It might be difficult to accept the fact that these possibilities do not exist and don't exist. You won't find out if you don't attempt. This section will help you'll be taught about the specific things you should and shouldn't do in order to make it happen with an attractive woman.

Unbecoming behavior

Before you can begin learning about relationships, you'll need to be aware of certain behavior you should beware of at all costs. If you engage in any of the behaviors which is discussed in this article you are very likely that you'll come off as creepy. It's the kind of behavior that could make women feel intimidated or feel uneasy with you. This is not what it feels like to be attracted as you're trying to test her boundaries. Here are some examples of this kind of behavior you should to stay clear of.

Don't start a conversation concerning sexual relations when you don't want to.

Don't share inappropriate photos or jokes that are inappropriate when it is clear that it will make her uncomfortable.

Do not stray from her physical boundaries by grasping her arm or putting her against a wall when you talk to her.

There are many ways to make you look creepy, but these are only a few examples. Be aware that women will have to interact with men in this manner numerous times in their lives. making it appear like you're one of them is the quickestand most effective way to convince her to take you out of her thoughts for good as a possible girlfriend or boyfriend.

How to Approach

The timing is important when you choose to approach women. A few guys are so focused on not appearing scary or threatening that they actually do the opposite and don't make an effort to approach women because they are afraid of appearing creepy. This is as harmful as frightening her away.

The interaction of meeting someone and speaking with them is not a creepy thing. Humans interact and come to know one another. There is always a place and time for every action and actions. You should use your judgement in these situations, as the idea of meeting women isn't always the best idea depending on where you are.

Location

If you wish to stay away from becoming creepy in a way, the first thing you have be thinking about is what's happening around you and in the area. For instance, walking up to an individual in a public space in bright, sunny weather out is different in comparison to walking home in the dark in that same area. In certain areas, such as bars and clubs patrons expect to be at least a little bit approached. But, outside of these specific places, women could consider it threat to let someone else come up to her at night. Don't attempt to impress anyone at the funeral!

Don't Corner her

Remember these points in mind when you are deciding to approach an individual. It is important to avoid engaging her in a trap or a corner regardless of whether or not you realize it or not. For example, speaking to a woman on the beach could seem natural, while talking with the woman at the small

Laundromat in your building could appear to be intimidating. Even if you're not trying the intention to "trap" her by denying her to access the door and blocking it by using your body will send the message in a subconscious way.

It's not a huge challenge to remember and is based on being aware about your surrounding, the appropriateness of the situation and the way she communicates. Do not become "that man" who keeps pushing regardless of the fact that she's not interested, and may even be angry at you. The social etiquette you use is crucial when you attempt to meet women. If a woman tells you "no," then learn to be respectful of it.

Make sure you have enough the space

If you're ever wondering if it's appropriate to be closer to someone you've have walked past or began talking to , or not It's an ideal idea to keep your own space. You should keep your distance, even if you're not requested to do otherwise. Make sure the woman has the right to leave the room when she would like to.

How to Approach

How do you determine whether you should be able to approach someone, and should someone want to be approached during a conversations with other people? One of the first signs you should look for is the way she moves. The body language she uses must be relaxed, calm and she should keep an upright posture. She may occasionally glance at her laptop or read to look around the room or look who are around her, or glance at what's happening outside the cafe. You may see her repeatedly glance at you when you are in the middle and that is a good indication that you are able to meet her.

Now that you understand that the spot is right the woman is browsing books during late afternoons at the neighborhood bookshop. You've realized that everything is in order and she's not cutting herself off from everyone else. It's okay to approach her and speak to her right today, which is straightforward enough, yet many guys are stuck. What should you be saying and doing? Do you have to touch her? Make a loud noise to let her know you are there?

When is the perfect time to inquire about her meet you again?

Reset your mind

The best way to approach this is to relax before you move forward. Do not get caught up in thinking enough that you beat yourself to the point that you are unable to talk, walk or think without a pause. It's just a matter of trying to speak to someone and overthinking the process is likely to make you look uneasy and send all sorts of odd signalling to her. Remember that she's human and deserves to be treated as one. Men often treat women as aliens. Don't be like this.

Moving towards

It's moment to make an effort to get closer and make sure that you don't sneak onto her. Make sure you walk up from her at an angle, and avoid approaching from the front. Also, ensure that you keep a safe distance from her, and do not hinder her freedom to move away or get out of the way should she wish to leave the situation.

Don't be concerned over the "lines"

A lot of guys get focused on giving their perfect "lines," but these aren't important.

There aren't many women who can remember what it was you told them. Don't get caught up in the talk about the perfect line for a pickup you hear in movies. The real world isn't a show and women aren't actors who play their roles.

If you are thinking too much about what you'll tell her and think about it more than the time you put into making the effort to meet her, you're probably making this a mistake. Remember that, even though the opening lines may not be so important as many people believe but you shouldn't simply walk up and talk to her however you like. Be respectful and try not to make her feel like you're being creepy. Making a rude or offensive statement immediately isn't going assist you in any way. Therefore, it is best to begin with a simple greeting and observe how things move ahead from there.

Be genuine

If you aren't sure the right words to use, just be sincere. You could say something like "You seem interesting, so I decided I'd meet you. Is it your first name?" Approaches like this aren't typical, they seem authentic and give you an immediate indication of whether she's keen on engaging with the person you are talking to or not. If she simply turns her attention to you, and then return to the things she was doing prior to it, this is an obvious sign that she's not interested to speak right now, and that you should proceed with your conversation. What is it like to meet an attractive woman and greet her? Then, you can attempt to talk!

Speaking to women

If you're a person of a certain type depending on your personality, you may find some success flirting with wit such as jokingly teasing women around. In various ways, it lets you to gauge the level of interest from both sides. For some it is essential to have a sense of humor and a woman who doesn't respond to banter or jokes is obviously unsuitable. In order to use this strategy it is necessary to know how to make someone laugh by being slightly mean, perhaps in the sense that you're doing your best to be friendly. To do this right, you must know how to behave as an older sister, rather than someone that you feel intimidated because of her appearance. It's about a playful style.

It's difficult for guys, admittedly especially if they're more private and do not show much attraction to women. It's not easy to get started if you haven't had much flirting with women.

Find her phone number

First, you must find something interesting that you can do before you attempt to reach her for her phone number. It is possible to ask her if you would prefer to have coffee at some point and then ask her if it is acceptable to contact her. If you've met just and you be interested in meeting her once more however, you must provide a date and location. It is also possible to suggest going out for a night out and provide her with your phone number. This will make her feel as though she has control and is in control of her choices. Whatever method you employ to win her attention ensure that your manner of speaking is casual and welcoming.

If, for any reason, she does not respond or rejects your offer in a blatant manner, you must be courteous and courteous. If you're demanding or pushy, you're an easy way to ruin your chances of getting her attention for good, and you'll never get her number.

Texting

Certain sources say that texting is completely inappropriate and that asking or calling for a date in person is the best method. However, the truth is that using text messages to ask for a date may be acceptable in certain situations and scenarios. It is not advisable to make a call because you're afraid or worried about calling her. In essence, you should decide on what she will like depending on her character, her age, and your perception of who she really is. The aim is to ensure that she feels as comfortable as is possible.

If you choose to message her Here are some points to be aware of.

Meeting

When you first message her, ensure that you refer to the first time that you and her had in person. You can prove that you pay attention and taking the time to remember the things you were discussing when you got together. You could, for instance, acknowledge her thanks for the suggestion she made for a movie or song or recall an incident that was funny the first time you saw her.

Be specific

In the next step, you must invite her to an event that is specific and at a specific location and at a specific date. Being clear with confidence is the best method to do this. If she's not available on that day but she appears to be eager to meet you and you want to offer her two dates, like Friday or Saturday, and you can ask her to choose the one that is most suitable for her. This allows her to choose her own day and provide you with a clear answer to your query.

Chapter 4: Discover Masculine Traits

The condition that defines the person as a man. It is a characteristic men have that are considered typical of men. Men have an aura of authority in the event that he possesses the characteristics of a man. Certain characteristics are linked to being a male and, often this is why women are typically vulnerable to in their quest for totality. If a man fails to show the masculine traits that are typically desired by women her, she can become apathetic towards him.

Charm as an Masculine Trait

It is the capability of a man an exuberance in a woman and alter the way she feels. Charm is not only a matter of the ability to make women smile through laughter or fun. Instead, it's about the character of an individual that could create a warm and inviting atmosphere and against which women can't defend her own.

If a person is charming is easily developing a sense of affection. They're missed because their presence is a mark. Their absence and appearance make an expression of their character and are occasions to cherish. Certain men can be quite abrasive in their behavior, while others are unassuming, yet are still considered as attractive by women. It is because they have this character trait as men.

If a man is charming, they're remembered and that means women keep them in their minds for a longer period of time. They become aware of that presence, even when they're absent and this begins to draw attention to women. They are drawn to being around the same type of man. They begin to crave the man. This is a great trait for a man when they need to make an impression when they are around women.

Charm should be effortless and natural. It is a part of the person's character regardless of the type of man he's. The way you treat people, whether sweet, cruel, or peaceful is not a problem. Charm can be yours. There are times when those who kill or commit criminal acts use charm as a cover to shield themselves from suspicion. This is due to it being an attractive characteristic which can easily drown women's senses with total attraction. The stories of women hosting serial killers without knowing aren't unusual. They have shared moments of their lives with a male who was psychopath and sadistic but charming.

Self-Confidence

Men must show qualities of self-confidence that will be seen by others as confidence. Most of the time, men do not doubt their identity when they realize that they're enough and are able to influence women to follow their ways. They choose what they want to and don't seem to to be pleasing to. A case study that was presented earlier showed self-sufficiency. A person who is in a lonely and isolated state and appears to love the solitude is an indication of confidence in their abilities.

They believe that the world is an object to them, and they are expected be able to attract the universe toward them. They don't try to achieve things through a struggle to be pleasing to. Instead, the person is calm and lives his life as someone who appears not to miss anyone , or have any desire for anyone. It is not always the case in the person as such. It is an example of being a bigger than life presence . One appears to not even notice the world around them. But, they are well-aware of the surroundings surrounding them, and actually they use this to communicate with and controlling the world surrounding them. Self-confidence is a way to prevent doubt and insecurity. Doubt is a deterrent since it can make one appear weak and frightened. However, women are usually reluctant to be subjugated to masculinity, and a man who isn't certain is subjected to the woman. This can cause women to show opposition, and, in the end she becomes complicated to the point that a man can't manage. Man must come out as an individual who is in control of the details of his life and is able to handle difficulties with his skills.

It must be noted that men are charged with the obligation of proving who they are. If the woman is believed to be impressed by the man's presence from a distance and maybe attracted to himduring the exchange the person has to declare that he was worthy to be taken notice of. The man shouldn't come out sluggish and unsure of the an interaction. He may be quiet or tense but his level of confidence must remain high. It's powerful and will smother any resentments of the woman. It is a way to empower the woman, especially the one who is stubborn. She stops fighting and wishes the man goodbye.

Being confident can make sure that the universe is working to your needs. It's about showing that you are at the top of your game and how you are not controlled by others. You don't play the victim and are invulnerable to any attempt to make you feel inferior, including the woman. This causes her to feel the need to be a part of this persona. She begins trusting in her man, under the false impression that she believes in him as well. A woman begins to experience life through your eyes. This is the reason she needs men. As an image screen, projecting her ideal lifestyle on her.

Speech and Eloquence

This is how to be a person of character. Man isn't obliged to be a fan of you because you are an engineer, lawyer, or doctor, or musician. She has to accept the qualifications that are relevant to her, and impact her. It's reasonable to think of that this is the reason musicians could take the wife of a doctor and the comparisons between the pay packets are not the only reason.

Eloquence refers to how you talk to her, and allow her to experience her desires for the future manifest. It's about making fantasies seem possible, and allowing her in a world that does not feel shackled. One must possess the ability to control and speak can be an effective instrument. To be eloquent you must be thoughtful in their words.

A majority of women overestimate their abilities and think they can utilize their own skills to intimidate a man. In the absence of being able to combat her with confidence and skills, she may cause feelings of anxiety and undermine the confidence of the man. It could be as detrimental as failing to meet confidence and confidence. and speech . This could mean it is a sign that she's subdued her man.

A speech must be made purposely to lead women to follow. Sometimes, it is employed to guide women astray, which could keep them on edge. This can make them feel a bit smug and at times, aspire to confuse her.

This is a great way to break her resistance to you. Don't think straight when you speak as this can make it hard to cut the flow of conversation from the sexual realm.

Speech and eloquence are but they are not about being chatty. It's about keeping an established way of speaking that excites women's sensibilities. For example, if you find a woman that does not feel confident in her abilities as an intellectual A man can sense his sensitivities. Then, flatter her intellectual abilities and tell her how you feel overwhelmed, not because of her exterior appearance but by the inner mind that lies beneath the exterior beauty. Help her to see her true self and, in doing so, she is attracted to you as she sees more of herself by your stimulating verbal messages.

Chapter 5: Factors You Should Be Educated About

I'm not going to sit here harping on the common and basic tips, but these are worthy of mentioning. I have seen a lot of males coaching men on ways to make women like their company, and they offer simple advice, and nothing other than that. The idea of explaining these issues without offering specific techniques which you can begin to suggest is not effective!

Let's discuss your body, and specifically the amount of fat you have. If you're over 25% body fat then the chances you meet women drastically different than if were at 15 percent body fat. Like I said before, looks do matter. Being overweight is something you can correct. Most women do not like overweight men. Of course, you've seen fat men have relationships with women, but I'm stressing the fact that your chances of getting a woman are drastically different in the case of not being overweight. Start engaging in a variety workouts and diets to shed that fat. The workouts that have proven successful for me have been the HIIT ones. It stands for high-intensity interval training. The workouts consist of intense, intense bursts then a brief break. These workouts require you to be 100% committed to your efforts. Regarding diet one that has resulted in success for me was the low-carb lifestyle. A low-carb diet which focuses on reducing the amount of carbohydrates. Foods like spaghetti, bread, starch, rice are all high in carbohydrates. Instead , your diet should be centered around protein and vegetables (such as beef, chicken or pork, and so on).). Additionally, sugar must be completely eliminated from your diet. In this way it is important to ensure that he has a moderate food intake. Even if you cut out the carbs, that does not mean you have to be a complete vegetarian as well as the meat. Being slimmer will greatly increase chances of connecting with women.

Apart from losing weight being in shape, losing weight will be beneficial. The development of muscle and an incredibly low fat percentage will increase your appeal. It doesn't matter what your appearance is when you have a low body fat percentage and strong muscles, you'll be above 60% of men in terms of looks. There's a whole idea that explains the process of building muscles. In the end, you need to get an exercise routine and begin lifting weights 3 times per week. Make sure that the last set you do is at a point of failure as well as be in the 15% caloric surplus to build muscle and take a good night's sleep. I suggest you start with your research if have a good understanding of weightlifting or the building of muscles.

Also, dress appropriately. It's not a good idea to dress for work, school or social events as if you're a 12-year-old. It's time to upgrade your look. First impressions are extremely important since as human beings, we form judgments based on the persona which is projected to us first. If you're wearing clothes such as basketball-style shorts (unless you're playing basketball) and shirts that have cheesy phrases on them baggy sweatpants, cargo pants, pyjamas tie dyes, and the like it will create bad first impressions. There are many styles that can create a stunning appearance. If you're going to work, dress in the suit and tie, sneakers and black pants and keep the look simple. A few great things you should be sure to have to ensure you're always in style for casual occasions include navy jackets, leather T-shirts, plain jackets black and blue jeans and a range of footwear, such as Chukka boots. There is no need to spend thousands of dollars for the best leather jacket. There are some decent leather jackets for just $150 stylish and will attract compliments.The same principle applies to navy jackets. There are a few affordable options with good quality that can make you appear stylish. Buy plain T-shirts in black, white or grey.Don't wear bright colors like yellow, pink or orange. For pants, there is nothing more casual than black or blue jeans. Finally, invest in a great pair of shoes , like Chukka boots. Also, ensure your fit correct and don't wear clothing that is too large or too baggy. For me, when I bought leather jackets I picked it one size larger than the norm since you need to have leather jackets which look sort of "slim and fitted". Alongside your attire accessories can certainly enhance your look a bit. The most important accessory that a man can have is a stylish watch. The best watches are expensive but , just like leather jackets, you can find cheap ones which look elegant. Additionally, you could wear the signet jewelry. A bonus tip: If you're looking to appear as if you're "rich" even though you're not, do not spend a lot of money on clothes that you wear every day, such as T-shirts. instead, invest a significant sum of money in things you wear daily like watches, rings and shoes.

Additionally, you can combine these items to create several outfits suitable for casual events. These outfits give a positive impression on your first date and improve your image as a male. These are some examples simple white T-shirt, blue jeans as well as black Converse shoes Plain black T-shirt and blue jacket blue chukka boots. A well-fitted black polo shirt paired with pants in blue and brown shoes; blue button-up shirt paired with black jeans. Many combinations can be created with the above items. Certain clothing items, like jackets, are suitable for wearing 3-4 days at a time.

Furthermore, you must consider three things before buying any of those products. Prior to that, you must make sure that the product's quality is excellent for the money. For instance there are leather jackets at $200 that come with high-quality Argentinean leather. Another factor is the to be fit. It's crucial. It is not attractive to wear clothes that aren't fitting you. Also, durability is important. Make sure you are aware of how durable the item is. For instance, plain white T-shirts last for one year before they develop yellow spots in the armpit section.

Chapter 6: Law Of Attraction And Dating

Many people are attracted by the concept of attraction due to its potential application in the realm of love. If you are in an open mind and are able to apply the concepts in the laws of attraction you'll be capable of turning things around with your love life. For you to begin with this, here are some useful ways you can make use of this idea to enhance your relationship.

A Positive Attitude

One of the first things you should develop is an optimistic attitude towards love. It's easy to hold on to negative , or even restrictive views regarding love. If you hold such beliefs that you do not want to be, you're reducing the chance of manifesting the love of your life. It is possible that you've got a positive outlook on dating. Do you frequently find yourself wishing for the perfect partner and dream about it? If so, it would do you good to spend some time to look at all the assumptions that you are making. Perhaps some painful events from your past have made you think that love isn't sustainable. Perhaps you're having doubts about the process of dating because you think that "finding your perfect partner will be a natural thing and the universe will provide you with an indication." The first thing to do is change your perspective to ensure that you do not let any negative or restrictive belief system to hinder you from finding women you are drawn to.

If you wish to keep an optimistic mindset that can help you create the love relationship you wish to have and want to create, then take the initiative to spend two minutes each day writing down your negative beliefs that you hold regarding love. For each belief you list down, you should make a list of the challenges that could arise and try to concentrate on the ones that are. For example, if think that "a relationship will always end in pain," change it to "when I meet the perfect person, I will be in a happy and satisfying relationship." It is important to decide to replace any feeling of inadequacy you hold regarding yourself with positive feelings.

The Art of Loving Yourself

It may sound a bit cliche however, it is vital to maintain an attitude of positivity towards yourself if you wish to make use of this law to enhance your relationship. By being self-conscious you give the wrong messages about what you desire from people. Your self-image affects your perception of other people. If you keep positive attitudes about yourself, you will be able to appreciate the positive things surrounding you.

Similar to any belief that is negative regarding love, you have to examine your past and your thoughts to address any negative impressions that you may have about yourself. Look at where the negative beliefs originate and the reason behind the similar beliefs. When you begin to write the negative beliefs that you hold about yourself, you can begin taking actions to correct the situation. When you write down your assumptions that you have, keep a record of the source as well as the positive belief you wish in place of the one you have. If, for instance, you feel that "I don't look attractive and therefore don't deserve to be to be a great friend," then dig deep to discover the root of the thought. Your low self-esteem could be due to the being bullied at high school. It is possible to replace this negative feeling by thinking something positive, such as "I have a beautiful appearance My friends and acquaintances have positive remarks regarding my looks."

Hold onto the Good

You have to be able to hang your faith in the positives of every date you have. It is likely that each date won't bring you joy and may not go as you expected. But if you take the time to recall the positive memories you have from each date, it can help keep a positive attitude towards dating. It could also help you gain knowledge that will help take you one step closer to finding the perfect partner.

When you go out with a partner and you are out on a date, it is essential to forget all your previous memories and not be concerned over the next day. Instead, you should become aware of the present moment. A thoughtful approach to dating can allow you to explore more possibilities. Additionally, it can allow you to enjoy yourself. When the date comes at an end you should come up with at least one positive thing about the date. Consider every date as a lesson. If, for instance, you feel like your date spoke often, instead of becoming annoyed consider that you have discovered the importance of being an excellent listener.

The nature of relationships can change naturally

As we've said earlier There is no reason to doubt that love requires the effort of a conscious person and energy. It is not possible to sit back and hope that your "one" to magically arrive at your door. If you let your mind sway into the future unnecessarily, and then create negative thoughts that may not ever happen, then you're essentially making yourself a victim. Think about it, and you'll discover that the majority of your anxieties or worries result from your excessive imagination. The laws of attraction suggest that you're affecting your chances of meeting someone by spending all your time worrying about whether the person you were with didn't like the company of. Instead of allowing negative feelings to keep you back, focus on other things and maintain your mind open and positive when it comes to dating. Be the best you can and then not worry about letting the dice fall wherever they fall.

Visualization

Doing daily positive visualization can improve your outlook regarding dating. Set a goal to devote at least ten minutes each day to imagine the ideal relationship. Make your vision as vibrant as your imagination allows you. Be aware of every detail that you feel when you're beloved and loved. Keep this feeling in your mind and let it flow through you. The principle behind that is called the law of attraction, it's to live in the present moment. The law of attraction basically states that you have to behave as if you possess what you want. If you act as if that you own something you want then you will get it in the near future! Try to make your visions extremely detailed. Focus on the feel, the sounds, taste and even the scents that you encounter.

Step out of Your Comfort Zone

If you are looking to increase your results in dating, it's an excellent idea to get out of your familiar zone. This is a standard behavior that is required for anyone who wants to make use of attract. Bring positive attitudes together with the determination to get out of your comfort zone and you'll have a recipe to be successful. You have to believe that you'll find the perfect person, and that there is someone waiting for you to meet them. Make sure you are curious and willing to gain knowledge in regards to the latest ways of dating, such as speed dating or getting set to go on an uninitiated date.

A Dream Board

Making a dream board is one way you can develop an optimistic attitude towards dating. Create a dream board for dating, and add images of what you would like your life with a partner to look as it appears across the wall. You can decorate it with clippings of photos or images from magazines that show your ideal scenario for dating. When you have created your board, you will need to put it in a place where you are able to look at it every day. You could also add motivating quotes and ideas to the wall.

You can allow your true self to Show Up

Laws of attraction can't be effective if you're not yourself. If you don't have the mindset of the person you truly are, you will never achieve what you want. When applying this principle to relationships, it basically means that you have to be open about your passions and stay true to who you are. If you're truly excited and interested this is when you're attractive. Consider a moment to think about it. Aren't you a little giddy whenever someone smiles at you? Also in allowing your real self to be exposed to the world, you improve your chances of developing a lasting connection with the woman you love. It's fine to be risky and let your true self to shine through.

Make use of positive affirmations

Make positive affirmations about dating in order to achieve your goals that you've established for yourself. Your thoughts can influence your actions and behaviors. If you focus on positive thoughts, you will see an improvement in how you behave. If you notice negative thoughts creeping in on your mind, you need to change the negative thought with one that is positive. Use positive affirmations such as "I am very excited and I am thrilled to get to know my partner" and "regardless of what happens I'll have an enjoyable time on the date." Positive affirmations can help you maintain an optimistic attitude when it comes to dating. The positive attitude of a person is quite contagious, and it could influence others around you.

Enjoy Surprises

Do not be quick to make judgments. This rule is applicable to every aspect of your life and dating is not an instance in particular. Do not make quick judgments about the people you meet during your dates. Even if someone appears appealing from afar, they may be a boring person. Be patient before you make a judgment regarding the person. It's great when you are clear of what you want from an intimate relationship. But, it's crucial to not eliminate someone from your life by not giving them the opportunity they deserve. The universe operates in a variety of bizarre ways and you'll never know what might come your way.

It is important to take a deliberate effort and invest some time working through the many methods you can apply this law to enhance your relationships.

Chapter 7: Confidence Vs Arrogance

In the final chapter we discuss the poor person. The one who is willing to sacrifice everything to please other people. This kind of behavior can be very harmful, and this is especially true since needy people aren't likely to be relied upon. But, many people who first hear about confidence, particularly the type of people who look on Youtube for information about it are likely to turn towards the opposite direction and this is arrogance.

Keep in mind what an arrogant individual appears like. They just respect themselves and not other people. Even if you believe that they aren't lacking self-esteem, you'll realize that isn't the case.

I'll present you with an example. A man is in need throughout his entire life. We'll refer to him as Mike to help tell the story.

Mike was never good when it came to girls. He was the cool guy with seven or eight girls he liked. However, these girls don't perceive an ally in Mike. He's listening for hours on how they've seen their boyfriend is a sly cheater their girlfriends or how much of the a** hole is he. After a few months , or perhaps years of this, he picks to get the confidence to tell them what he thinks of them. However, he is snubbed by friends. After many years of suffering and rejection and resentment, he begins to hate women. "Why did she not like me. I'm not a failure I never fail to teach them that I want them to feel safe, I love them, and I am sure that no woman will ever accept me".

He decides that there's no need in giving women respect. He set out to make each woman is around him feel like they're not worth the time because they're not valued as they must pay attention, be loved and respect him. Therefore, the next time you visit an establishment, he will talk with women who have no interest and will make comments like:

"Your hair looks bad" or "you have too much puffiness"

After a few rejections, and after a few drinks are thrown at the face of his friends... He found a woman who is interested in him. They start to get together however... rather than trying to meet women, he focuses on spending the time playing cool and pretending that she's the only one to do the work. They do end up becoming a couple however after a few months the man stops playing. He had already found a girl who was willing to take him to bed and treat him like a queen, and... what's the point. Two more months passed and then, following another argument, the two broke each other. It's a wrap this time.

Mike will message her or phone her hundreds of times, making excuses and telling her how much he cherishes her. However, there's no sign of improvement. She doesn't want any contact with him any more.

The issue with Mike's behaviour is that he transformed from a petty personality into an overly confident one. He blamed girls for his shortcomings, when actually, Mike was the one to be the one to blame. After he changed his mind and made girls feel like they didn't matter and he was not attractive, he did not change. He only had a handful of girls with a negative background, and likely have issues within their family. A father who was abusive or a mother who was not loving the girls.

Then, those girls discovered the love of Mike the perfect escape, an opportunity to forget about their troubles which is why they would sleep with Mike. Since they were treated poorly by their parents, these youngsters have been raised to think that this is how they deserve to be treated. They allowed Mike run over them because they were afraid of his departure from them. But once Mike is losing the show, his needsy personality came out and, then, well. The girl was the first to cross him.

It's the reason why an arrogant man regardless of whether he meets girls, would like to be able to enjoy a good time with girls. It's better to be single than to be in a bad relationship.

The way you treat your partner can determine the fate of the man. If you're involved in an affair, and it's not one you love it will make your life more difficult than it was before. A partner is someone who is able to share everything that you go to the feelings they feel. If you choose to take a partner who makes you feel unhappy and you feel bad, you'll be the same for them. The loop will form. I prefer calling it "The miserable loop". If it's formed you and your companion will begin to have more bad times than good ones.

I'm not saying that all relationships are perfect, but every relationship has its difficulties, some of them really wonderful and in an occasion, such as the one I share with my partner. However, our relationship is filled with happiness and love, it has been a struggle since we began it. That doesn't mean that we do not struggle.

We build our relationship on a solid foundation, built on love, trust, and loyalty. We can overcome the differences that we have and solve many of our problems.

The law on investment

If you like my previous examples and think that it was okay to do the approach Mike did because it can aid you in sleeping with girls, then please bear with me for a while because I'll explain the reasons why this occurred.

The way in which first attraction is created between two people happens when we believe that the person we are with is superior to us. So, we would like to spend time with that person since we believe that they will make us feel satisfied. We don't have the ability to determine what a person's worth is. We cannot look up their bank accounts or determine what a good family man someone could be, so we must use our senses to judge the extent to which someone is of greater value than we do. I'm using the term "values" for the reason that it's more in line with the purpose I had in mind and not mean that you're less valuable than others. In this case, value is the term I use to use to describe a person's charisma confidence, self-esteem, as well as overall excellence. There may not be better people than others, there are certainly higher-quality people than others.

Then, when Mike made this girl feel that she was unworthy, he displayed that he was not as invested in the opinions of that person and, as a result, the person he was a better fit to her than she was. If he did this to the girls who threw an alcoholic drink on his face and spit on him, he was deemed as a snob who was not worth the effort, and these girls did not have any interest in his character. Why?

It's because the girls were high-quality girls who knew that Mike was not worth the money for them, and that's why they care.

Be aware that the motives behind your actions are more important that the words you actually use. When Mike said to the girls that they were ugly but he didn't mean that he was saying it, he just wanted to make them feel bad. Since some of the initial girls were very good and admired him, they resisted him because they were aware of the motives behind his actions. When the shy poor-treated girl was reading the same words she believed she didn't merit more, so she accepted the treatment and was attracted to him since the guy showed less commitment.

Let's discuss my situation. Let's suppose that a person known as Dave was dependent all of his life. After completing his high school days, he read an article titled Models that talked about honesty, confidence and how to attract the right partner by simply being yourself. After two relationships in which there was no way to find his spot, mostly due to the fact that the relationship did not follow the guidelines in the book , and was still in need of. He began to hang together with one of the peers. He was not looking for an affair at the moment. However, he was able to grow by being honest and self-confidence and when hanging out with girls, he began telling her stories about himself as well as his past, good stories humorous stories, sad stories. Dave shares his worries with her and confesses that he gets sucked at things. After a few months, the two became best friends However, there was something more. They began to become friends.

In the time that Dave was out drinking with his ex-girlfriends Maya Dave's former classmate and now his best friend were concerned who called Dave to ask whether he'd like to visit her house to do his homework. This is the moment that Maya realises that she really likes Dave and was unhappy that he was seeing other girls. However, since Dave did not want to be in a relationship, she wasn't sure of how to proceed. After a couple of days, Maya realized she had to leave in the event that summer would be over, they'd most likely never get together.

At an evening at Dave's house After a few drinks, Maya was hesitant to share her feelings with Dave and revealed to Dave her feelings. He was thrilled that he was in love with Maya as well. The reason he chose to not inform her of this was that he had put the subject on the table for a possible relationship. He was astonished at how a girl could love him enough to risk rejection in order to have him. In the end, women don't need to be able to do that. That's why these two bonded and remain together at the time the book is written.

What differentiated Dave and Mike is that while both demonstrated to girls that they were less interested in them than however, they did it in a different manner. Mike was able to make them feel guilty as Dave admitted his own insecurities stories, his experiences, and things girls can be giddy about. Dave made them feel happy and by sharing things he normally do, he seemed less engaged. It's a bit counterintuitive I am aware. However, it does work.

This is the reason why honesty is so important. In the next section, we'll discuss how to be a trustworthy and honest person.

Chapter 8: How To Say And Not Say

No matter what your norm or the type of date you take part in, and the efforts you put into preparing prior to the date, all it will go to waste if your unable to impress your date. What better way to show it off on your initial date, than by impressing them by your impressive conversational abilities. It's not a known, but it starts with a conversation. The reason for this is simply amazing. an easy message, even a few words, could be the catalyst for something better. No matter what you should always create an impression with the way you conduct the first meeting with your date. It is possible to miss out on a chance to meet someone you really love simply because you messed up on your first date.

What should you say during your date:

Breaking the ice is the first step:

"How long ago did it take you to arrive? I'm sorry for keeping you in limbo."

This is a classic opening for those who are late to the next. This will break the ice between two of you. In addition, you can say sorry, and expressing your regrets is highly appreciated by the person you are dating.

"What were you doing prior to arriving here? Was it a problem with the traffic?"

The idea of asking about the day your date spent together is also a great way to start off the conversation. It allows both of you to exchange couple of lines, and from there you will be able to feel and establish the tone of your conversation over the entire time.

"How was your work experience on your end? Have you had a good day at work, or did you have a terrible day?"

Being polite enough to inquire what your date's plans were for the day was at work is the ideal way to start a conversation. It gives you something to discuss, a subject that is important to him her, and could go for a long time. In addition it shows how much you're worried about the mood of your date.

"How did the traffic flow this time? My route was quite lucky as I scored three greens in one row."

If you are honest or not, traffic can play a significant role in the date. Why? It is because the first thing you really think about when you're driving to your date is traffic, not your date. It is a secret prayer to God to avoid getting stuck in traffic, because of obviously, you don't wish to be late and make your date wait. Asking about the traffic situation as an ice-breaker is sure to bring you to the same level and any awkwardness will go away.

The most secure topics to discuss on a date: If you've established the mood of your relationship, it's generally recommended to discuss some subjects that are easy, topics that allow you to learn more about your partner. Be sure to ensure that you don't look as if you're trying to gather facts that aren't appropriate to your partner. Make sure you stay clear of these to help your date go smoothly. Also, you don't want to share too many details about yourself on your first meeting. This can make you appear desperate and that's not the way you prefer to be seen looking. Before you expose your worst behavior you should stay away from topics that will get you talking.

Movies:

If you're going out on a date with a movie making a pre-movie as well as a post-movie review can be a great conversation start. A good pre-movie chat will include your expectations about the film and a small portion of the synopsis, as well as the scenes you're eager to watching. A great post-movie discussion will include your first impressions of the film in general and your most memorable scene or portion of the film, as well as your overall impression of the storyline of the film. Make sure to allow the conversation to be casual and receptive. You can ask your date questions such as "Did you enjoy the movie?" or "What do you think of the movie?" This will help to have a conversation that flows and is significant in the same moment.

If your date doesn't require a film viewing it is an ideal conversation topic on your next date. Many people, if certainly none of them, has watched one or two movies. This is a popular moment for many people. In order to spark an interest in movies, you can try these conversations ideas:

"What kinds of genres of movies do you like? Comedy, romance, suspense, sci-fi? Are there horror films? "

"What is your top film? We could watch it together. That would be a lot of enjoyable."

"Who is your favorite actor or actress in all of time? My personal favorite is (name your most favored actor or actress)."

"Did you watch the most recent film by (name actor or actress)? It was praised by the Internet. Are you interested in watching it in the near future together with me?"

"Are you a Marvel fan? What's the latest Marvel movie you've watched? It was mine (mention the most recent Marvel movie you've watched)."

Food:

Let's face it: people live for food. It is said that food put it is heaven and the essence of life. No one is against food, and that is simply absurd. There are a variety of food items that people take pleasure in and love. Everyone can have something to discuss food. This is the reason a conversation about food is sure to get you talking to your partner. It is certain that this is a very engaging discussion once you begin to discuss food.

The best method to have an enjoyable discussion about eating is to be aware of what your date and you like and don't like. This will help you discover common foods that you enjoy and could provide excellent date ideas for the future. Additionally, it will bring about a exchange of ideas and thoughts about food , which can lead to an interesting conversation. Here are some suggestions that could make this subject an effective conversation starter

"What kind of food do you enjoy the most? Are you a burger person? What about pizzas and pastas? Are you a rice person?"

"Are you a fan of buffets? I absolutely enjoy the one at (name your favourite buffet restaurant) because they offer 10 food stations. It's by far the top!"

"What is your most favorite restaurant? My favorite is (mention the name of the restaurant). It's near the (mention an address). They have the best ribs around town!"

"Do you enjoy (mention the name of a food) food? I know of a restaurant that offers the finest (mention your name for the the cuisine) food available in the city. It's so delicious that it is packed. Let me know if would like to visit so that we can make reservations in advance."

Travels:

When you talk about travel, you appear sophisticated and well-educated. It makes the person you are dating think that you are someone who is well-traveled, diverse and well-travelled. Being exposed to different cultures and the beliefs of the places you've been to really help you think about the world in a different way. This can instantly entice your partner and make them want to ask more questions regarding travel. In this way, the two of you will engage in a meaningful conversation, where both of you will benefit from one another's experiences. Ask your date, where has been in recent times. This will definitely get the conversation moving. You could also ask another follow-up inquiry about the activities of your guest during the travel. Do not forget to ask him or her overall impression of the location. It is also possible to share a tale of your most memorable trip.

This can make the conversation more engaging. Here are some topics for conversation on travel:

"Where have you been recently? Where was it and what was your experience?"

"Do you enjoy traveling? What was the last destination you visited that you truly loved?"

"Have you visited (name the last place you've visited)? The waterfalls and beaches are truly unique. You must definitely visit the area."

"What are your thoughts about (name the place you would like to visit)? I've heard lots of great travel reviews for this particular place, and I'd like to visit in the near future."

"Do you like adventure? What kinds of nature excursions are you most interested in? I absolutely am a fan of the beach, as it's just so serene and makes me feel relaxed."

Current and newsworthy developments:

Another great topic for conversation are current news stories and events across the country and around the world at large. Be sure, prior to the date, you've at the very least researched the major current events that are making waves within the community. This will make you appear as an individual who is constantly current and up-to-date with the latest news. Consider these topics as the basis for your conversation as this could allow you to talk about a wide range of different topics. But, make sure you do not be too political or religious. It could be a problem for your partner in a manner that you don't wish to cause any harm.

To avoid situations that could lead to discrimination, it is always possible to ask questions that are general and secure. Make sure your questions are wide enough to expand the conversation since this is the intention. Keep the conversation focused on positive news and events because you don't want the mood on the event to drastically change simply because you're talking about gruesome and sad incidents. It is possible to use these questions to start an opportunity to start conversations about news and current happenings:

"Have you heard about the latest ploy our president pulled to promote his election? What do you think of it?"

"What are your thoughts about the Freedom of Information bill? It's been generating the awareness of people lately and I think that the administration should approve the bill. Do you agree?"

"Did you have any idea that President (name one of the presidents of another country) is scheduled to visit the country in the near future? I'm shocked at the chaos caused by his motorcade will be passing by my office."

"I I am so excited to see coming up with the idea of a Papal visit to our country. I believe it will be in January for a Youth Congress. Did you know about it?"

"Did you know about what went down at this Republican Debate last week? What they never resolved was the cute person who was behind the moderator. It's unbelievable."

Pop Culture:

It is also crucial to know the most recent trends and topics concerning pop culture. Nowadays, people are obsessed with the latest trends and out therefore, it is essential to have an understanding of you are asked about a topic that isn't part of the discussion. It is not a good idea to be a victim of the impression that you're an old-fashioned person. Here are some ideas for conversation ideas for the ever-controversial pop culture.

"Have you attended the fashion shows of this season's New York Fashion Week? What were your thoughts about these fashion events?"

"What is your most fav style of fashion? Your wardrobe is always stylish. Always up to the mark you know?"

"Your shoes look very nice. Where did you purchase them? I haven't seen them on the streets here."

"Have you seen the latest sneak peek of (mention the TV show you and your partner like)? I'm so excited about the new season which will be released in October."

"Did you see the latest episode of (mention the TV show that your partner likes)? I was watching it on the TV the other night. It definitely got me interested in this particular film."

What NOT to say during your meeting:

To ensure that your date is successful, make sure not to discuss these topics and discussions:

Exes/Past Relationships:

There's really no need to provide reasons for you to avoid the subject when you are on an evening date, especially if you are on an initial date. Don't be a jerk. Your date isn't concerned about the relationship you had with your ex and their love for them because they'll view you as threat or an opponent. Also, you don't want to find out about their previous relationships. It could cause your date awkward and tension-filled. In addition, if you've got nothing positive or positive to share about your ex-love you should remain silent since you don't wish for your date to imagine themselves in your previous love's situation. This could make your night miserable.

"I know this is weird but you really do look and dress like my ex-boyfriend/girlfriend. I find it extremely amusing and hilarious."

"You will not believe what my ex-partner has told me today. She contacted me on Facebook because she knew I was planning an outing with you. He/she was so envious and she literally begged me not to meet you for dinner. So immature."

"I am not sure the reason I was wrong in my relationship before but. I was convinced that we were the perfect match for one another. We rarely had arguments. Oh well we fell out."

"You really have lovely eyes. They're blue. They're just like (name your ex-girlfriend or boyfriend)."

"Oh My God! My ex-boyfriend/girlfriend had the exact same shirt as you. Is this funny?"

Money/Finances:

Discussions about financial matters or the topic of money in general can be very unsettling to nearly every kind of person. It doesn't matter if it is discussed positively or negatively, it is still money , and many people feel it is not appropriate to discuss on dates, particularly when it comes to money. However, there is no need to be concerned because this is among the subjects that is easily kept out of the conversation because it doesn't appear frequently even in casual conversations. In reality, how much you earn and the sum you own should not be discussed during dates. Even those who are married and long-term partners struggle to discuss financial matters. Therefore, make sure you keep this out of your life for an extended period of time.

"I have lost $2,000 today due to my deal was destroyed by a company that came from nowhere. This really upset me because I wanted to make that deal so badly."

"How how much you earn in your job? I'm considering moving to your company as I feel that I'm underpaid at (name the company you work for). I don't like working there anymore."

"Dinner is mine since I received an increase of $100 per hour in my position. I've been waiting for the raise but now it's here, I'm celebrating."

"This restaurant is very expensive. They are expecting me to spend $78 for that steak that was not at all like a steak? I will never come to this place again."

"Do you have any idea that I earned $2,500 for the day? My agent helped me negotiate the best deal and guess what? They paid me directly on the instantaneously."

What are you "looking at" in an intimate relationship:

It's a common question that is asked during every date. In reality, many people do their best to avoid asking this question to their date or to themselves whenever they meet the first person they meet. But it will always come up one way or the other because everyone wants to know? It is often thought of as a way to protect themselves because knowing immediately what you both are seeking in a relationship is an insurance policy. It will not let couple waste more time together after you have a quick idea whether you can or aren't able to figure it out. However, it is recommended to stay clear of this subject matter, especially if you've just started dating since you could be sending unclear signals to your partner that could or may not bother the other person up. To ensure your safety, take your time and enjoy each other's company, and then continue to move on from there.

"I am keeping this checklist of things, right. It's sort of like a list for the person I'm planning to meet. The person must be more taller than me, naturally. Physically fit with beautiful body. In particular, attractive. You're definitely on my list of "must-haves."

"I dislike to be around someone who isn't independent, because it completely makes me feel uncomfortable. As a 23-year-old I'm completely by myself and that's the type of person I would like to be with."

"Do you do you love Maroon 5? If not, I will swear to my life that we're never intended for each other. This is the way I cherish them."

"Do do you belong to a certain kind? I'm curious, however because you are my kind, but I might not be able to fit into yours. Would you like to pass this with me?"

"I realize it's an early start for this. But, I'd like for you to go out on a regular basis every Friday to this place. I'd like to make it our routine."

You, constantly:

A one of the most important aspects of dating is discussing your personal life and sharing some information about yourself to the person you are dating since getting to know one others is the aim. But, looking as if you're listing a lot of adjectives to describe your self is a big turnoff. It doesn't come across as being humble. Remember that showing is always more effective than telling, as actions speak more than words. Don't say that you are funny instead let me smile. Do not say that you're beautiful, but instead, let me discover the beauty in myself. This is the essence of being who you are and the results will surely follow over time.

"I am bored in situations where I have to be in the edges of a particular project. I don't like having to feel that way. This is the reason I don't want to be in the limelight every day."

"I know that I'm not supposed to be telling you that, but I got promoted this morning. Actually my promotion was so unexpected that I was not expecting to receive it at all. I just got promoted this month. I am shocked."

"I would like for myself to take the lead who plans the next date we'll be going to have. Relax and unwind and let me handle all the planning. I don't need you to stress out. Let me handle it."

"I am not sure about it, do you. Everyone in the office is talking about this new system installed. You know, guys, I don't need to keep repeating my story and explain to them how it's accomplished."

"I love going to (name the country) next month , because I always want to return. This place was meant to fit my life. It's just amazing."

There are plenty of different topics you must avoid when meeting for the first time, particularly with your partner. A few of them are religious and political issues that could be extremely controversial for anyone involved in this. Be sure to stay clear of these topics in the best way you can in order to ensure a pleasant day for your.

Chapter 9: Becoming Your Strongest And Best Self

In addition to the most important methods that assist you in finding the woman of your dreams and establishing an enjoyable relationship The knowledge you gain from this book can help you enhance other areas within your daily life. It will assist you in becoming your most attractive self.

A friend once told me "Thomas I don't know why you're not getting along with women. You've got the looks as well as the money, a great job and more. I'm not even close to what you have and I'm broke too But you can see how wonderful my relationships with females are." He added, "If I had what you have, my love life would be insane." My friend was right.

He was an expert with women, able to attract any girl he desired. There were times when he had several girls who were being drawn to him as a guy who was broke and staying in his home, with mom. I have seen girls travel across the country to meet him.

My friend had an many women around him and would often introduce a few of them to his buddies.

My friend has seen numerous gorgeous women fall in love with him , and he was in debt, but he wasn't spending this much. He would often tell me, "Thomas, it's not always about money," which was absolutely right. He once shared with me the story of the gorgeous woman he had dated who would make payments for date nights and engage in everything to attract his attention. I learned much from him.

We must understand the reason why many men have a difficult time dating.

1.1 What's the reason that men have a hard time with women and what it means to be your The Best You

Men struggle with women because they're not at their very best and this is because they have a limit in their minds that holds them from living life fully. In order to attract the woman you want to be with in your life and wooing her in a proper manner, you must come from a place of determination.

What happens in your head when you view a gorgeous woman walking on the other side of town? How do you feel in your brain when you spot an attractive woman in the street, whom you'd like to meet for an evening date? Do you meet her in person and engage in with her or do you pause in thought?

A lot of men are comfortable speaking to women whom they're not drawn to, but once they have met an attractive woman they truly enjoy, they're not their true self anymore.

The majority of men view a gorgeous woman as superior to others They then place her on a pedestal, to an extent that conversations get difficult and due to the invisible radar that all women are equipped with, they will dismiss the guy fast due to his weakness and unconfident. The first time you meet women is crucial. If you do not make an impression that is positive making her see as a possible romantic partner will be difficult.

The majority of my relationships that I have had success with that I have with women were ones in which my first impression of them was excellent. In courtships, where I appeared fragile and insecure during our first encounter regardless of what I later did the relationship did not go well for me.

I typically advise people to quit after failing in the initial or second interactions. This will save you much time, energy and energy. If you're struggling to find the woman you've always wanted is because you're not your greatest and most confident self.

How do you improve your self?

1.2 1. What You Need to be Your Best The Most Strong Self

Your journey to becoming the most effective and most powerful self is a journey of self-transformation which begins by embracing your own growth and, in this instance involves the following:

Be Whole

Desperation and neediness are to be very ugly. If you're desperate and desperate, no matter if you do date her, she'll eventually leave you. It's not necessary to have a girlfriend to feel comfortable about yourself. A man with a purpose is a handsome man. You should strive for a full driven, purpose-driven existence!

Do things that give satisfaction and joy and provide you with a sense of wholeness. Are you living a full life? Without anyone to tell you that you look good Do you feel fantastic being someone who is trying to improve themselves?

Don't put women on pedestals as it can make you feel less than in the presence of gorgeous women. A feeling of inferiority is a huge turn-off. Be proud of yourself and love yourself and believe that you are attractive and worthy of the woman of your dreams.

Believe in Yourself and Develop Self-confidence

I've had several male friends who appeared "challenged in the area of looks" however, they are also engaged to beautiful women. What I have noticed in these guys was their self-confidence. If I was in presence of one and before he even approached an attractive woman the man would ask "Do you see the girl in the corner? I'm planning to approach her and get her to date."

Based on this mindset, men are not contemplating "how or if" it's going to work with his girlfriend, no He is considering "when" the girl is attracted the court and eventually the girl. These men are the exception, not the norm.

However, for most men, when they are captivated by a gorgeous woman the first thought that pops to mind is of "being rejected" or that the woman is outside of his realm. In the wake of this thought the man experiences the exact outcome thought of and that is the woman turns him down. Are you aware of the reason? Since he is operating with an insecurity of self-worth, the person is with the assumption that a gorgeous woman will never want anything to do with him. A man who is in this mindset will see himself falling short long before even attempting. A man like this is not able to find the woman of his dreams.

It's simple to recognize how your mind or thoughts might be negatively affecting your life and impacting how you have to say to women? This aspect of your life is one I strongly suggest you to improve on as mastering this skill will allow you to be more successful in your relationships with women and will prove valuable for other areas that you live in.

Be a "Nice Guy."

I see the term Nice Guy as a weak man with no self-esteem or self-esteem. A nice man is someone who doesn't take a stand for his own or what he believes or what he is looking for and who lets others take advantage of him. He is a young man in a mature male body, and a person-pleaser.

I was a very Nice Guy. From what I've learned the art of the definition of an extremely Nice Guy doesn't work with women. If Nice Guys are trying to win over women, they usually perform the following actions:

They're not explicit with their motives and their feelings.

They are scared that they might make mistakes and make mistakes or be at risk.

They are scared to approach a woman directly for sex.

They fear hurting the feelings of a woman. Due to this, they are reluctant to speak up that they ought to say which is why, as a result the things start to pile up.

They'll do things they don't want to do to please women.

They provide to women with expectations (usually in indirect ways) and become angry and angry when there is no return.

They aren't standing on their own and fight for what they would like.

They are also accessible.

Women have a powerful sense of smell which quickly detects Nice Guys. A lot of Nice Guys like to buy women things. By nature women are awestruck by gifts. They generally accept these gifts in exchange for the fact they are they will be the "nice guy" is placed in the"friend zone. The nice guy may be devastated and wonder why he's so nice to her, however they don't really want to be to be romantically.

1.3: How to Develop Your Best Self

A woman would like an individual who is trustworthy and confident and can go to what he wants with no worry. For women, the term "nice guy" means Nice Guy is weak and ineffective. If you meet women and start to treat her like an idol, you're creating a trap for yourself to fail If you do this, women won't find yourself to be attractive or genuine enough to be able to get married.

In order to become your most authentic self, the moment you first meet, or begin dating the woman you've always wanted:

Always express your true feelings and desires

Inform her early that you're looking for her. Be honest with her and make it clear your motives from the beginning. This alone can be sufficient to alter your relationship and dating life for the rest of your life.

Men who are looking for an affair with a woman with a romantic inclination approach the process in a manner which causes women to befriend the man due to not sure of his intentions.

It is best to be upfront about your expectations to be able to easily determine what she believes and then move ahead if she doesn't. If you aren't upfront, you could end up committing yourself emotionally. If she does eventually turn off your offer, the process of resigning be much more difficult and painful. If you're likely to fail, you should fail early , and then go on to the next woman who is available.

Be Vulnerable Guys

The power of vulnerability is in the ability to overcome it. Be prepared to fail. If you'd like her to send you naked women request it. If you don't like her way of treating you, let her know. If you are interested in her and want to be with her, let her know. If you are looking to create an impression to her, let her know. Be vulnerable. To elevate your relationship to the next level, you have to be vulnerable.

If You're Looking for Sex Request It

Women are also attracted to sex as some do more than males. If you're with your spouse and she doesn't like you in bed, inform her. Tell her that you want to know why. Gentlemen are scared to ask for this, and wait for her to move which rarely occurs. Women want you to role of the leader. You are the one who can do it.

Don't be too eager to please her

If you are not happy with the way someone has been treating you, let her about it, but with respect. Let her know even if you think that she might not enjoy being told. Do not allow the situation to grow. If you keep allowing the way she treats you, she'll continue in this manner. It's part of taking action to defend yourself. I've done this to some women, and I gained the trust of these women and respect.

If a woman isn't able to appreciate you, she won't appreciate you romantically. Women will not regard yourself as her rock, or feel secure around your presence if you're unable to take on her. If she's treating you as a 'young man and you're playing it safe, she'll not trust you. And If she isn't confident in you, it's hard to get her to trust you romantically. It's a shame that this is exactly where Nice Guys fail with women. If women try to try to test their strength and fail, the women feel dissatisfied.

Let me share an example of a moment that I have experienced in my life. There was once a lady I was interested in and she could tell that I was attracted by her. A few days ago, she texted me a text message stating that I was invited to visit her office and assist her with printing. Not knowing what to do, I left my work place to visit her and assist. When I entered her workplace, she told me, "You came quickly."

While I thought I was being nice to her by swiftly providing my help She saw it in a different way. She felt that she was directing me, or acting as if my desire was to be a good person. What do you think? I was not able to achieve any success with her. There were many other instances when I did not pass "her test" too. All women are tested.

Don't be a People-pleaser

Be yourself and refrain from doing things solely for the purpose to please her. Make sure you are true to your words as well as let the actions reflect your words. This is how you earn respect.

Let's suppose you're planning to go to a soccer match at 2 pm when your girlfriend tells her "Baby Please join me to the mall at 2 pm" and you leave your football game in order to be nice to your lady by fulfilling what she demanded of you. Although she may initially express gratitude however, it could lead her to question your masculine side. Gentlemen are often confused as to why they do whatever women asks for and are always there for her, but she's getting smitten by a man who isn't doing any of these things. They feel miserable and depressed. The problem is that the guy who is not approaching her from a position of strength and this will make him more attractive to her. He's not an "Yes" type of guy.

The lesson here is you must be doing things to please a woman because you know that it's the right thing to do so and not just to impress her. If your instincts to be masculine dictate that you to do this, then be honest about it, but don't take it on.

Don't give to women for the reason that you're who you are, not because you believe that it'll make her love you or cause her to want to have a sexual relationship with you. If you're doing that you're deceiving yourself and making yourself vulnerable to suffering and loss. Don't be a slave to any condition. Give genuinely.

Always stand up for yourself

If the woman you're interested in isn't willing to talk to you once you've expressed your interest and desires then walk away. If she doesn't reciprocate your the desire, then walk away. Unfortunately, many men keep "pursuing" women, even after she has clearly expressed her disinterest. In continuing to pursue, you're open to being a target for disrespect and could cause her to reject you more.

A man who believes in himself that values and loves his own worth, and who is able to show self-esteem will not pursue women who don't like him. The pursuit of too much leads to being rejected. I once had a romantic relationship with a gorgeous woman who claimed she had changed her phone number as she was constantly chasing guys after her with a ferocious. She told those who were interested that she wasn't interested however they wouldn't take it seriously; they kept coming at her with a ferocious. They would call her constantly. Due to this, she decided to change her number.

Don't be too available to Her

You should have a life beyond your girlfriend or woman you're interested in. One of the mistakes guys make is once they find a woman they love and fall in love with, they neglect other areas of their lives like interests, studies, friends and goals, their purpose and more.

They begin spending most of their time with their girlfriend. This isn't a effective way to build relationships. While spending time with your lady is crucial, don't place her in the center of your attention or pay her constant pay attention to her.

Enjoy Your Life, and Do Things that Bring You Joy

Do not wait for a woman to enter your life to be content. Find yourself your happiness. Many men believe that if they have the woman of their dreams they'll be content. If you think this you're not, then you're lying to yourself.

Many are married but they are also they are miserable. There is no woman who can provide you with happiness. First, be happy. Find a happy, single. A person who is happy is beautiful and real happiness is a result of inner.

Accept Daily Self-Growth

Keep on growing physically, mentally spiritually, as well as financially. You can always improve your performance daily. Do not allow yourself to come to the stage in your life at which you're not growing anymore.

If you follow the guidelines mentioned above in your daily routine and you'll become the best version of yourself. I urge you to do the effort, focus on yourself and learn to become an expert in this field of life. Being your most powerful and best self will benefit you in other areas as well.

Chapter 10: What Should I Do The Next Date?

The first date was great. You spoke openly and truthfully and were a reflection of yourself as a person. The relationship was positive and you shared an emotional bond. You are comfortable with one with each other. You like her. She evidently likes you.

So, what are you going to do next time you meet?

This is the when most men start making elaborate plans for getting a woman's attention. Based on the information you've read thus far you're probably not likely to fall into this trap. This isn't the time to make elaborate plans. Now is the best time to...

Do the same thing you normally do

That's right. Do not change anything. In the second as well as the subsequent dates, you'll want to live your normal life and stay the same you've always been. Why should you change your appearance if she likes you so much that she wanted to go on another meeting with her?

You contact her. You get a call from her. You've had a conversation since your last meeting. What is the time before you can meet again? It does not matter. You're focused on your day-to-day activities. What do you think you should say on the phone or in a text message? You're not the only one to answer that. You're the one who made the relationship. She is a fan of you, much more than before. Keep being you.

If your second date is within a day or week following the first date, you're just going to do the things that are suitable for you and your partner. If you'd like to be together on the next day and you have the time without having to change your day-to-day routine, do not hesitate to have your second date on the following day. If you're unable to make time for your next date then you must be the same honest and honest person that you had on your first date and let her know that. She will be able to understand when you have previous commitments, and can understand if she's got previous commitments.

If it's time to discuss what you'll do for your second date, do the same thing you'd normally do on the day, and invite her to be a part of your plans. If you're washing clothes take a few loads of laundry and share it together. If you're watching your favourite television show, ask whether she'd be interested in watching it along with you. If you're thinking of doing some exercise or going for a run or taking your pet for a walk, going for an excursion, or shopping or anything else, invite her to be a part of your journey.

You've got the picture. Follow the steps you had planned to do Invite her come along.

It's the right time to continue exploring and consolidating your connection

She wants to keep exploring your world, and you'd like to explore her. If you're both happy with what you see this will only increase your relationship. It doesn't require a lavish dinner to establish a connection.

Casual, daily routine dates are the most enjoyable since they create a healthy relationship between you and your lady. She will see that you're never trying to fool the woman in any manner which is crucial. If you're honest with your self and honest with her, she'll be able to see the truth.

Before we move on before we continue, I'd like you to recognize that there is something. What I've explained here is what makes you distinct from other guys. You're not just a guy. You're a real person. I don't care about anything you've read or heard previously. I've witnessed what happens to people who employ deceitful techniques of persuasion. If it happens just a few days into their marriage, or two years after they've married the relationship always crashes and burns. The people who blindly adhere to these "gurus" will only set themselves to fail. Thank you for making it this far into the book. You're the one.

Continue to explore

As long as she is still exploring your interests, you should be looking into her further. You're trying to determine whether this woman is someone you would like to associate yourself in. That's why keeping up your normal routine and having dates that aren't overly scheduled or designed to impress her is crucial. You're letting yourself explore if your relationship together can continue as you are a an integral part of one another's routines and daily routines while keeping an honest and open dialogue is the most effective way to do this.

Chapter 11: Learning To Play The Game

Have you heard of the phrase "having games"? It's typically used to refer to a man and signifies that the guy knows how to seduce women. For most men, seducing women is just an opportunity to play. As with any game, if you wish to win, you need follow the rules and beat your opponent. There is a woman-friendly variant of this game. And when you play it right you will be attracted by any man you pick.

In the bar - It all begins at the bar, and how you play the cards here. I have mentioned only revealing one part of your body at time, as you want to maintain the mystery. This is also true to the details you share about your self. Men are enthralled by anything that is a challenge such as a riddle or an anagram mystery. They love to solve problems and are willing to work for it. The more difficult they must be at it, the more interested and attracted to them.

With this important information in mind, be sure you keep an aura of mystery surrounding you, your location or relationship status. This will make men shiver since they'll be unable to understand why you don't reveal more. What's hidden about you? Why don't you reveal all the details? They'll be enthralled and totally fascinated.

After the night, whatever you decide to do, make sure that you don't head home with a man from your first evening. Actually, don't offer them your number initially. If they truly desire it, they'll fight for it. You may allow the person you love to take through your front door, but not anything else. He's not allowed to leap between your sheets like the other. Except if that's what you're looking for.

If your goal is to spend the evening and forget about him, then go ahead. However, if you're looking to hold his attention longer and have him wanting to keep coming back you'll need remain patient, and be a test for his endurance in addition. Let him know that just buying him drinks at the bar isn't enough to convince you and show him that you're worth more. Much more.

If he rings - Now you can take advantage by the possibility that you have the power and can extend your "suffering" to a bit longer. If he calls, and he'll call, do not answer the first attempt, allow him to try again. If you do call, don't agree to the date immediately. It's not your day to be busy when that he makes a proposal and he'll have to try again , or make his plans around your schedule. He'll be eager to find out what you're doing constantly and it'll take a toll on him throughout this week until the day he is able to meet you. Congratulations, you've successfully and safely sunk your "claws" into his.

On the day - So you've finally scheduled an evening date after a lot of shifting around, and things are good. He's charming, funny and smart. He even pleaded to cover the cost of dinner. Score! Now you can go home you think? Wrong! You're giving him a kiss goodnight on the way out. In no way are you going to let him come to your house to you for the "drink" or any other reason. You must get your foot in the ground and secure it into position.

Do you know that The Rules advise not sleeping with a man before 3rd date? Consider that advice and follow it because, whether you believe you me, it does work. There's a reason many women are awed on this method and it's because you keep trying to keep stalling, and men appreciate it. Some will say that it's frustrating and makes him insane however if then, what is the reason he's still in this position? I'm sure He is definitely there, even at this moment.

The relationship was a success – You got it! You convinced him to commit. Now, what? The game has to end there, right? Wrong, again! Keep him on your toes. If you're looking to keep your attraction going and remain the main player in the relationship, continue to surprise him on a daily basis. Don't allow him to be able to ignore you and don't let him down. The key is to ensure that you know that you have options available and that you'll take them into consideration in the event that he doesn't treat you with respect.

Why is this working?

There are those who doubt regarding the probability of success this technique has. However, to fully be able to understand the reasons the method is effective, and what it does, you need to be aware of the way that men's brains function. People are drawn to the thrill of the chase and are attracted by anything that is interesting. The human brain is trained to be able to think of solutions (this is the reason they have mathematical abilities) and anything that represents an obstacle (whether you're building an IKEA closet with no instructions or navigating to their location without a map, or finding a girl who is unpredictably) is sure to keep their interest.

The game is a favorite for men and believe they're experts at playing however, what they don't realize is that they enjoy it more when women are superior in the game than they are and ultimately win. We all desire things that we don't get, but for men who aren't able to achieve it, the impossible has the unique appeal of. This is why if he doesn't feels like he's got you in his hand, he'll take a bite out of yours. Of of course, you don't need to be an ever-present ice queen You can be a little more flexible. Don't let routine get between you, and ensure that you're always making things exciting and surprising. So, you'll remain intriguing to him. Your relationship will never be dull vibrant, fresh and thrilling and you'll always be irresistible to him.

Chapter 12: Volume Dating Like A Winner

I'm sure it's been clear to you that the sport you're involved in is known as "Volume Dancing." It's all about the volume. It's about processing a massive amount of people in a brief amount of time. It's crucial to comprehend the fundamental rules for bulk dating. If you believed that you're already a volume-dating person when you're receiving responses on the internet Wait until you begin getting to know them in person.

Speed dating is very well-known across the United States for a reason. The average person doesn't have the luxury of time. In the same way it is important to realize that you're not afforded the time to enjoy the luxury of going out for date nights with the guys. He. Wrong will continue to remain the Mr. Wrong regardless of how you spend time with him, and no matter how many times you keep in touch.

It is vital to keep these suggestions in your mind.

Remember that you have the power.

Remember that men need your attention more so than you do. I know this may be extremely difficult to believe, particularly when you're feeling alone, but it's the reality. Statistics show that the majority of dating sites online are like sausage factories. There are so many men as compared to females. If you look at it from the standpoint of supply and demand the numbers favor you. Utilize this advantage to your advantage. Never get desperate. Be sure to keep in mind that they are more dependent on you than you require them. There is no one worthy of being a cause for concern.

If you believe you've met the right guys, the chances are high that there's a better person out there. Make this your primary guideline. If you don't, you'll end up kissing a lot of Frogs, hoping that one of them would become prince.

Get dressed to impress.

When you're out for one of your many large-scale occasions, it's easy to dress in an un appropriate manner. It's like, "Wow, I'm getting all these dates. I'm probably going to look like a slob because I'm basically the men I'm interviewing." Don't give in to the urge and dress to impress.

It is important to realize that it's a dual-sided road. If you want a man to be attracted to you, and the most important thing is to remain curious about your appearance, you need to present yourself as something that's worthy of keeping. You need to appear as something worth fighting to achieve.

It is a battle to be in love. It demands some kind of competition. It's a whole lot of trouble. If you dress as someone who is a slob, it's not difficult for him to conclude it's not worth their effort and effort. I'm hoping you can have this. Make yourself appear like a prize. Make it appear like you're worth the effort. In addition your appearance is a reflection of the amount you appreciate yourself.

If you dress as an obnoxious slob, you don't value yourself this much. You may think you're not worth it. In the event that these could be messages you're giving to men Don't be shocked if they won't be able to respect you. I hope that you can understand how this plays out.

It is also important to keep in mind that you are able to create expectations for your appearance. Your manner of dressing and the accessories you select along with the outfits you select will all set the tone for expectations. Every aspect of your appearance sends signals regarding your school and your beliefs as well as your dreams and hopes as well as your priorities and many other important aspects.

It is important to dress so that you give clear signals. It's not that I'm saying that you have to dress as if you're not. What I'm suggesting is that you must at the very minimum dress in a way that reflects your best expectations.

If you've put in the effort looking nice You can expect the same level of effort from your date. This is a very helpful point of advice for those who are having recurring dates. It's not a good idea for your date to look attractive on the first date, and later appear like an absolute disgrace the following.

This is the first filter for dates.

The most challenging date is your first day. It's hard because women have difficulty let go. They face a lot of difficulty getting out of the house. Just like the filtering of online content, I provide the same advice Do not be afraid to be brutal. Don't be afraid of calling it quits when you're not having fun.

It is important to realize that dating is about you, at the very beginning. When you're married that's the two of you. However, in the beginning the focus is on you. You must keep your head in the game. You're no Mother Theresa. You're not there to make people feel special. You're not contributing to making the world better by making it easier for people who don't merit your time. Be confident in making the decision.

If you think that in some way or another this person does not have it, then that's fine. It's totally up to you. You don't have to do this person any favors. Maybe he invited you to a restaurant with a posh name but don't be obligated to go to do it. Instead, always remember your mission. Your aim is to feel relaxed.

If you're comfortable with this guy, it could be something going on. You won't be able to fully understand the truth until you've spent time with him. This brings up my next point of advice: Don't overdo it. If you're out on dates, don't be tempted to think that you have to wait until he's spoken about certain things you have to take to the next level. Do not rush it. It must feel right and all it comes down to your degree of ease.

If you feel he's worth keeping Let him know. The same goes for you it isn't a good idea to drag the process over for too long that the individual ends up getting mixed messages. I'm sure I've said earlier that these people require more from you than you do them. In the same vein, never undervalue the ability of guys to manage many things going on simultaneously. They're constantly exploring new possibilities.

It's crucial to make sure you tell a guy whether you're looking to keep him around. Men don't like women who bluff around. Although a amount of mystery goes far however, you shouldn't go overboard. There have been many instances of women who tried too hard to be able to obtain that they couldn't obtain. Why? The person just got bailed out. Don't let that happen you if you believe you've gotten the right guy.

Quick body language primer

If you're in a conversation with someone be sure to consider that you're not talking to them via words. They're not only listening to the words that come from your mouth. They're also looking for non-verbal signals. Face expressions, voice tone, how fast you speak your posture, the speed at which you speak, and even your body language speak more louder than the actual contents of your words.

If you're reckless or careless in your body language or nonverbal signals, you may lose people you'd actually be satisfied with. Take note of your body communication. Make sure you're communicating the message you intend to convey.

Signs that you're interested

If a woman is attracted in a man, she does not move her arms. The most common posture is that shows her wrists or she stares straight into the direction of the man and reveals her neck.

In the world of animals every gesture of wrists and neck can create a sense of vulnerability. If a person of the other sex shows the same to you, this indicates that they're genuinely comfortable with you. In the simplest sense it shows that they're at least interested. Take note of these signals. Be sure to forward these messages in the event that you're interested, and be prepared to pick up the signals when you filter your dates.

Indicates that he's in

If a man is attracted the tone of their voice shifts and they are more likely to lean inward, with their wrists exposed. There's less displays of dominance, such as hands placed on the hips, and crossed arms, with thumbs hanging out. Instead they lean forward with legs that are open, and the chest is extending.

Based on behavioral studies of primates primates show their chests, it's an intentional display of vulnerability since it only takes one strong strike to the chest to cause serious injury to the primate. When males show this behavior without any other indicators, it suggests that they are attracting a lot of attention.

The secret?

The key of body language lies in the ability to send signals back and forward. If you notice that the person is interested, make sure you show that you are also in the same direction. The frequency with which the signals are moving around indicates that there is a mutual desire. If you observe that he's altering the messages he transmits back, it's a good idea to examine the signs more closely as you may be interpreting way too closely, or it could be a false positives.

Do not place yourself in a scenario that you simply jump on the first positive signal because it might be an untrue positive. If it's constant and consistent and consistent, then you're onto something, particularly if you constantly bounce around the signals between the two.

Pay attention to the other non-verbal signals

Apart from body language, people communicate through facial expressions, voice tone, and even mannerisms. There are many males who display an intense level of passion and excitement when they begin speaking quickly. It is important to focus on these various aspects and put them together into an overall.

It is important to keep in mind the fact that there will be a point during the process, if there are contradictions in the signals, that should be your signal to pause. If, however, the vast majority of signals indicate one direction, then do the right thing.

Chapter 13: Making The First Impression And Ensuring It's The Last

"What I'm looking for is the initial impression. I'd like to share what the people see when they first enter the room. What my eyes see when I first look at it."
-Pierre Bonnard

The ability to make a conversation that establishes you as attractive and charming on the first date is what everyone is seeking. However, few people are able to do that and the majority find themselves in the back of the party, where they envy those who are socially enthralled.

It is not uncommon when your conversational skills aren't up to scratch and your throat is swollen up whenever a woman is standing in the front of you. It's more frequent than you imagine. A lot of men struggle to talk to women in one-liners or even having lengthy conversations.

The fact is that having a good talking makes men more appealing to women. It is essential to learn how to engage in a lively conversation in order to increase the chances of meeting with the lady you're loving.

How to Make Conversations? Art of Making Conversation

Modern-day dating and excellent communication skills go hand-in-hand. Because there are a variety of ways of communicating these days, it can be a challenge and sometimes words be lost in meaning.

Additionally, misunderstandings can be created due to the fact that implied meanings are used in various contexts and. In this age of social media, it is not preparing the Generation Y as well as Generation Z to have a appropriate conversation with others in person or online. While they have phones throughout the day they do not like being called and prefer tweets, text messages or emails.

If you're looking to get married, you've to learn how to converse and, if you don't, on the date, you'll only be paying attention to the woman as you nod your heads, which as the previous chapter explained in detail, does not make a good impression on the girl. You will end up having an unpleasant date since she believes you're not attentive and is trying to find the right answer.

It's an exaggeration, and does not have anything to do with actual-life dating However, it's very close to the truth.

The art of dating and the art of Calls

A lot of people believe that in-person conversation is more important than phone calls and that phone calls aren't the right way to talk. This isn't necessarily the case particularly when it comes to relationships. Telephone calls are a fantastic method to determine if the two of you share any sort of chemistry. If you and your prospective date don't share the same preferences and have no shared personality traits that can cause you to connect. In this situation, the communication is pretty obvious during the call and you'll be able to quickly go back to your original plan without having to meet in person. This can be difficult if you decide to give up on meeting later. It is also possible to learn to converse properly in phone calls without having examine the person as it can be confusing and is a major cause of poor communication skills.

A Good Listener

Being able to converse well doesn't always mean speaking well. Being attentive to your partner's speak is an essential aspect of conversation. asking the appropriate questions and making comments that keep the conversation going is what a constructive conversation should be as: a two-way road. Find out what interests your date has and establish a more intimate relationship, thus avoid going down the same path of rehashing lines and boring discussions.

Trouble in Paradise

Approaching women and engaging in a conversation isn't a huge hurdle to conquer, as it is for some guys. It is, however, an actual issue that can be an obstacle for men in their search for love. There are a variety of reasons for this and they differ between individuals. Every person has the exact reasons why they are unable to speak to women. Some women are intimidating to them which is why they do not attempt to meet them or even have had bad experiences in the past and have quit.

Simply No Problem

A man posted online that he is having difficulty talking to women since women do not bother to talk to him. Furthermore, he doesn't bother to make conversation for himself, since he's not certain if women actually want to talk to him.

That, naturally is where the problems is. They don't bother to engage in conversation, only to feel resentful toward the other sex.

Fear of the opposite Sex

Men are often at a disadvantage with women as they are afraid of being publically criticized if they meet women. This is the reason that causes men to not try their luck at bars and at parties.

The fear typically takes shape following a series of unfortunate teenage interactions with girls who do not like males and be nasty to them later on about it. No longer are you no longer a teenager. Adult women are not able to humiliate males in public with no reason. Keep a respectful line of separation and try it out. Someday you'll surely win.

Natural Instincts

It's normal to have reservations when speaking to someone of a different gender. If this is an option that women are afraid to speak to males and asking them out.

Their motives may not have the same logic, but the fact remains that their reluctance and desire not to approach men in order to inquire about their sexual preferences isn't the same as yours, and will give males a certain amount confidence.

Conversation with the other gender becomes easier as we get older. As as a teenager, teenage girls were probably similar to the wicked witches of Disney movies, but then you began to socialize and meet people when you were older. It was easy to speak to women, particularly the ones who you did not find attractive. All you need is a little courage and practice and you'll be able and ask them to meet.

The Shy Guy Dilemma

The shy guys feel that they're at an end of their barrel in regards to looking appealing to females. It's not true at all. Women are said to be drawn for shy guys because they're gentle and sweet and they feel more at ease with them. The issue, however, is that shy guys face difficulties speaking with women.

To look more attractive, the primary aspect is to keep an excellent hygiene. If you are well-groomed and fresh it will make you feel confident about yourself and your confidence will increase automatically.

Try to encourage others Smile at strangers, and make sure to give compliments to strangers. This will increase your sense of self-worth and make you feel more worthy.

There is no doubt that you look attractive to women, as women love shy men. The most important thing is to look attractive and feel comfortable of attracting women.

To improve the skills of communication, you can try practising before an mirror and use what you've learned to a female. There is a chance that you will fail at first, however it isn't the end of the road.

Tips and Tricks to Convert

Be on the lookout for Signals

You don't need to go up to an unintentionally random woman you love in an establishment when you think you're not confident enough or confidence, and your approach could come back to you.

Find clues and hints in the behavior of women and determine whether they're attracted to the person you are or not. It's generally pretty simple to tell if you are attracted to someone. For instance, If a woman glances towards you with a smile, that means she hopes that you will meet and speak to her.

This signal should boost your confidence, as the woman loves what she believes in you and is looking to share it with her. Avoid women who appear annoyed or upset or who appear who is busy or distracted. It is more easy to engage with women who appear attracted to talking with you.

Do not overdo the Icebreaker

Be simple and avoid some flimsy pick-up phrases. They will not help to break the ice, but they will likely make you feel embarrassed as you'll end up being rejected.

There are women who have experienced all sorts of pickup lines, but they aren't effective therefore your strategy should be an easy "hey" to open the conversation. Then, you can make use of your surroundings as a opportunity to discuss something which could further advance your conversation.

The Conversation is on

The icebreaker phase is just the beginning. If you can make it through that stage you'll have to begin a conversation in order to be more prepared.

Take a look at a sporting event of the day before or check out the news to provide you with an understanding of the national or local events. These are great ideas for an opportunity to start conversations and, if you can convince her to be interested, it may suffice to maintain an ongoing conversation.

More than a conversation

Sometimes, a simple conversation isn't enough. Yes, you've got the attention of your partner, but you're no longer suffering from nervousness. It's much easier to take it a step further and assess how you are doing with your efforts to impress her. A few games that are fun and entertaining can work wonders when you are in a situation where conversations are flowing and you're friendly and the games don't need you to begin a new conversation.

For example, playing a game of tic tac toe where the loser is required to hand over their numbers to the winners an exciting way for you to meet each other and put yourself in the spotlight. The next step is to decide whether she's willing to swap numbers or not.

Most important you need to accomplish is to make an impression that is lasting. The only way to make that happen is by beginning conversations and having confidence. If you're not sure you can try to fake it. For a time forget about being the shy guy who is having trouble communicating with women. Then, attempt to make yourself appear more attractive. Your first impression can determine your chances of picking women up or even break the relationship.

Chapter 14: Language Of Flirting: 25 Phrases Women Love

From the moment you begin communicating with her on the internet to the time you schedule the date for a meeting, you'll need to create excitement, chemistry and attraction to ensure that she's eager to meet you. If done in properly is the most effective way to achieve this.

As you already know what you should say -- and not say -- in the messages you've sent her This chapter will arm you with a handful of feminine phrases women love and should use when it is natural to you:

#1:

"I would like to ..."

The way to finish this statement can be done in a variety of ways. For example, you can write, "I would love to hear your thoughts on the subject"X,"" as well as "Phone conversations are undervalued today. I would like for you to share your thoughts."

Whatever way you conclude the statement, it is effective effectively because it conveys your sincere desire to meet her. It is an exhortation that will get her to open up and speaking with you.

#2:

"I am aware of ..."

Similar to the first one it is possible to finish the ellipsis in a variety of sexually attractive ways. For example, you can write, "Your bio says you like warm hugs, so I'm sending an incredibly warm hug to soothe you after a tiring day at work" or "I believe you're an avid Star Wars fan. There are two tickets to the movie "Star Wars: The Rise of Skywalker". Are you interested in joining me?"

In both cases you're letting her know that you know that you would like to get to know her, expressing your enthusiasm and showing her that you are interested and in the last sentence, you are inviting her to the manner that she is likely to decline, especially in the case of a genuine Star Wars fan. Furthermore, this is a encouraging statement that you can utilize to initiate an interaction that creates trust and arouses.

#3:

"How do I ..."

"How do I make you smile this night?", "How can you bring a smile on the face of your friend?", "How can you make you feel loved?", or even "How can I assist you?" are all great examples of how you could make this statement a way to play with her.

The reason this statement is effective is because it demonstrates that you value and you are an emotionally intelligent man since it is only an emotional intelligent man could be concerned about women he hasn't seen.

#4:

"By my way I'm still wearing that smile you showed me the first time we spoke."

Remarking in a nonchalant way about what she does to make you feel (such as the first time you spoke to her or connected on the internet) can ensure that she is happy about the impact she's made on you. Don't be afraid to tell her!

#5:

"Are You on ...?"

It is possible to finish this with a variety of different ways. For example, "Are you on Facebook?" lets her know that you'd prefer to join a different dating site. This helps to build rapport and chemistry because it indicates that you are eager for the relationship to develop further.

#6:

"Do you use ..."

Two examples of this are: "Do you use Cleopatra's beauty regimen? Your smile is just too breathtaking and your face too radiant", or, "Do you use social media?" The first message is smack-you-in-the-face flirtatious. It lets her know that you've observed her gorgeous smile and facial features that will make her feel comfortable. The second part is more subtle. It indicates to her that your fascination with her has increased and will bring positive feelings to her.

#7:

"Our online chats brighten my evenings. I'm looking forward to the day when I can look into your eyes as we talk the night away."

Simply mentioning how much you like chatting with her can bring out her happy hormones. Insisting that you can't wait for the day that you're comfortable enough to look each other in the eyes while you spend the night chatting will make her feel you are looking to build an authentic relationship.

#8:
"Talking with you was in my thoughts all day long."
Simply mentioning how she's thought of you can convey how interested and attracted to her, leaving her feeling appreciated and wanted.

#9:
"Has anyone ever told you? ..."
As a prompting word that you can make this phrase in a variety of ways. You could, for instance, ask, "Has anyone ever told you that your smile would make rainbows an opportunity to compete?", or, "Has anyone ever told you how stunning your red-colored face looks?"
These two statements will make her feel fantastic They will also convey your genuine interest in her.

#10:
"There's nothing more I'd love more right now than being together with you."
You're telling her that you've considered having a relationship with her -- you are making her feel more confident about the possibility of becoming "your person"and after pondering it, you're not looking for

anything more now than right now. This kind of statement could make her feel "all-gooey for you in the inside".

#11:

"Your ___."

It could be "Your smile is what drives me nuts," or "Your witty banter is something I enjoy every single day." Whatever it is by using this phrase, you let her know how awesome you believe she's.

#12

"Do do you recognize what it is that I admire about you the greatest about your personality?"

Saying that you are in love with certain aspects of her character is a fantastic method of flirting, stirring sparks of attraction, create relationships to keep conversation moving.

#13:

"Tell me about the most memorable experience you've had."

On first look it may seem like a flirtatious gesture. This is because it is a sign that you love her enough to be curious about the aspects that define who she is. And, further, the desire to be aware of the things that make her feel can help create intimacy.

#14:

"Every when my app for dating contacts me I check it out in the hope that it's coming from you."

Let her know that you are looking for getting to hear from her will make her wanting to speak to you even more since she understands that you appreciate it.

#15:

"How are you doing?"

Alongside saying that you are quite fun and take an interest in what she's up to This message also has an undertone: you're asking because you don't wish to join her in doing whatever she's doing. "How you doing?" is also a important question that could cause all sorts of sexually entangled conversations.

#16:

"What's your list of things to do and how do I be a part of it?"

The first aspect this message conveys is to inform her that you are able to be fun and silly and women love men who are able to make them laugh and don't think too much about themselves.

It also will let her know that you'd like to be an important part of her everyday day life (the "To-do lists" reference) and creates an impression that you're looking to establish a lasting connection.

#17:

"You have been in my nightmares the night before."

"You have been in my dream the night before" is a wonderful method of letting her know how much she enthralls you and will likely make her more enthusiastic and also open the conversation for flirting. The most common response to this type of message is "Oh? Tell me what you've dreamed about."

#18:

"Let's play an exciting game of coin toss. We'll do something that you enjoy this weekend. Tails I buy you dinner Friday night."

In the first place, you tell her that you've got a fun streak. The second part of the message will let her know that you're keen to meet her which can help increase the chances of attracting her.

#19:

"How do the the sound of a drink tomorrow night?"

The most powerful phrases and questions like this one can let women be aware that you're ready to go for it meet her in person and engage in a one-on-one discussion that is you are ready to take your relationship off the table.

#20:

"Since we both love to take food, I don't see why we shouldn't share the same meal (or a dish you both enjoy]."

This message is about removing things from the internet and moving forward with the relationship this is great because text messaging has its limitations in terms of knowing people and developing a strong emotional connection.

#21:

"What's your most enjoyable weekend-time activity? And when do we have to take it on?"

If you ask her about her interests and let her know that you're open to discussing these interests with her, you are someone she's comfortable spending time with and that's an excellent thing for both of you. Addition of "when could we meet" is a subtle method of telling her that you want to have a conversation with her without the use of a dating app.

#22:

"Tell me about your dream first-date."

Simply letting her know that you're thinking of "her debut date" can be enough to convey that you'd like to share one with her, and to make it happen in a manner that will fulfill some of her romantic fantasies of first-dates.

If you want to add some hot sauce to your message, you can include, "and the best time to come to you to thank you." This lets her know you're keen to be a part of her goals and dreams as it lets her know you're interested in forming an authentic relationship.

#23:

"If you agree to eating dinner or watching a movie with me or going out for drinks and so on. I'll let you be my friend."

As well as being fun and sassy, this message makes her think about what it's like to spend time together with her hands in the open, crying in the boyfriend and girlfriend.

#24:

"I could see me falling in love with you."

In telling her about how you could imagine yourself being to her prompts her thinking about what it would feel to be being in a relationship this is a great thing since it lets her know that you are determined to turn what you're going through with each other into something more substantial.

Chapter 15: More Information About Dating

Have you been aware of the good guy concept of jocks versus good boys? This idea is based on the idea that the best guys always come in last, and how jocks always get every girl. This is real and happens often. But, if you are able to think about this idea you'll notice how different relationships are between jocks and good guys. Jocks are a source of power and adventure that can be appealing during the initial few months, but it also has limits. At some point, women discover how selfish and stupid their jock-lovers are, and then they decide to leave and look for a new one. On the other hand the best guys offer the security and comfort that are thought to be girlfriend material. So, if you're hoping to hang out and meet an attractive woman for one night, then you are the jock. But, if you're someone who would like to be in a long-term relationship, you must be the kind of guy. Learn to respect her boundaries and how to let her prevail in your disputes.

If you don't become too possessive and demanding of your partner, you'll be able to build an ongoing relationship.

Be aware that dating a woman can be very difficult, especially if you are the first to search for one. It is important to know how to be more persistent and be constant when it comes to dating. The majority of women prefer to try out the waters before they meet a man. They'll inquire about a variety of questions concerning your life, your interests or even about other subjects. It is crucial to keep a consistent attitude in your answers. It isn't a good idea to begin a relationship based on lies. It is more beneficial to inform her of the truth about your profession and your interests, or everything in between.

If it's time to go out on an evening out, you have be sure to dress as a gentleman. Learn to get the door open or when to sit down. Be respectful of her choices and don't attempt to force her into doing something you would like to do such as having sexual relations. Be more respectful and allow her to decide. If she is at ease and is not offended by what you do If she is, then you stand the best likelihood of getting her as a boyfriend.

The process of courting and dating is essential to be successful in getting an attractive girlfriend. The first date you'll have is the introduction phase. In this stage she will examine out your personality and attempt to get answers regarding your personality and life. If she is satisfied with the information she receives then she'll accept another date, and later to a third. After an additional date odds of getting her attention are extremely high. At this point you may possibly even touch her. But, if you decide to kiss or even touch her, first you need to be aware of indications. There are always a few indications to look for before kissing her. If you decide to make her kiss you and she accepts and you are happy, then congratulations! You have become her boyfriend.

When you are dating, you must be aware of the importance of giving gifts. The majority of dating sites advise that you give gifts of high value. The gift of expensive items should not be considered as it could be a sign that women are aware that you're trying to win their love. Instead of purchasing expensive jewelry or other luxury objects, just offer her chocolates and flowers. If you are meeting women at bars, do avoid buying women expensive drinks because buying those drinks will not only empty your pockets but can also make you appear like a shopper for women.

Finally, there are some rules you must know about women. The majority of women believe that men should be in their comfort zone, while some think you're an individual with advantages. If you're interested in knowing whether you're in a relationship or are simply friends , then ask her. be able to communicate with her to know what she is thinking. If she doesn't like the person you are with, then you should move on. There are many women looking for a new partner to meet. But, if she says yes and you're now officially engaged, take the time to learn to love and respect her to ensure that you'll be in a relationship for a long duration.

Chapter 16: "Finish Strong"

What you do with your evening is what determines the confidence of the next date or any other when you leave it unfinished. Whatever the way you dress or flawless the entire evening was but a bad ending could ruin your chances of a subsequent date. Also, all the efforts you put into to make that date happen will be wasted. This aspect of the date is extremely important and should be considered as important as the preparations that are made prior to the date.

"Do you wish to listen to something sweet? I thoroughly enjoyed this evening. It definitely was one for the books. I'm sure you were feeling the same way as I did."

"Thank for your time tonight. It was really nice seeing with you face to face. You're just as hilarious in person as you are online. I hope you enjoyed yourself as much as I've had."

"I enjoyed a wonderful evening this evening with you. The food was delicious. The movie was fantastic. You were great. Thank you for taking the time to spend some moments with me. I hope that you had a blast."

"I really didn't think I would find you to be as amazing in person. You are so amazing. Your actions to help those children. It's very nice to meet an individual who not only is concerned about her immediate family, but also those less fortunate as well. Thanks for sharing your story."

"I am having way too much fun tonight with you. However, I don't want you to leave too late. Could I take you in the car? This is the least I can provide for you."

"It's closing in and I do not want delay you too all night. I wish we could have more time to spend together, as I really loved your company. Goodnight, and be safe I'm sure you're fine."

"I really wish that this night didn't be over. It's been a while since I've experienced this much joy. It's also time to have a date. I hope that you feel the same way and I hope I did not exhaust you with my endless stories. Goodnight!"

"I'd like to learn more about you as I find you to be interesting. Are you free next weekend? We might be able to do this time and time again?"

"I know of another restaurant which serves your favourite dish. It's totally outrageous and delicious. We must definitely try it with each other since we have the same taste. Contact me anytime you are in the next week."

"I didn't realize you were a fan of"the Fast and the Furious series. We should definitely watch it together since I've been wishing to see it for the last about two months ago. Please let me know when and where is do you mind?"

"You are aware of this? You're a very interesting person. I really enjoyed having conversations with you. I'd like to know more about your job and family. Let's do it once more, okay?"

"I really want to see you for a second time next week. Do you have time, say on a Saturday night? Another restaurant ought to try close by. I've heard it had excellent reviews during their first week."

"Do you wish to travel to another place this week? What are you looking to do? I'm up for any and everything. Let's eat dinner together and do something afterward. Do you feel up to it?"

"I was told there's a great Indie film due to be released at the cinemas this week. I'm sure you're into films like that. Would you like to have a the movie with your partner?"

"I didn't realize you were into swimming as much as me. It's really weird to request a girl to go on one of our swimming dates, but since we love it so greatly, would you like to give it a go? I'm free next weekend. Let me know what you're planning to do to help us plan."

"I really want to hug you. Do you want to?"

It is important to have fun when dating however, it must be planned with care and executed in order to be as a success. Don't forget that a bad date could end up destroying your chances of getting your "right" date. Make sure to adhere to these tips and reminders to ensure pleasant and memorable dates.

Chapter 17: The Hints Are For Riddles.

I'll go over conflict styles in the future however I believe it's important to start with this particularly since a lot of men tend to identify themselves as the conflict style but doesn't necessarily address the issue in a clear manner.

If your approach to conflict isn't explicitly confrontational, it's acceptable. The majority of people's styles aren't.

If everyone were 100% aggressive as well as direct in their approach, it's likely that nothing could ever be done without some throwing of plates and temper anger. The world requires every type of conflict to solve its many issues There is no single style that is perfect or even the best.

However, whatever you prefer to approach conflict that suits your personality most, you will be able to manage to be quite clear and not be passively aggressive with the negative emotions you have. This requires becoming less apprehensive about the idea of confrontation , however I've discovered it's more an issue of rethinking your notions behind the reason you're saying something rather than hints at it.

There are no conflicts or disputes These are just occasions to enhance your relationship and communication. Making a fuss about things can lead to missed opportunities and the prolongation of problems. The idea of defensiveness is not appropriate in a relationship focussed on improvement. What's the primary goal when defensiveness is the dominant factor?

Do you really want to rely on your female partner to recognize your subtle signals even though we know women are often blind and insensitive? Are you really allowing your relationship to unravel when you express your displeasure over how she handles the dishes? And so on.

Naturally, the idea is far more easy to state than executed. It's obvious that the best way to proceed is to speak it out and not hint at it but it's an act that requires confidence and security when confronting. However, the process gets easier the first time you've done it (and it's cathartic) and you realize that the sky isn't falling and your relationship remains remarkably intact.

By not mentioning it, the idea means that there will be less misunderstandings among you and your partner... as well as also fewer irritations for you when she isn't picking clues that you believe are obvious however, they aren't.

All of this results in more efficient and quicker resolution of conflicts that reduces anger and builds a feeling of respect and equality towards you.

Let's just be adamant to disagree.

Some of the most important or most significant conversations are capable of appearing as zombies. You think you've finished however they continue to persist and return to haunt you, because you didn't kill them correctly.

The majority of the time, this happens because problems haven't been addressed in a satisfactory way. However, guess what? There are some issues that will not be whatever you would like them to be or how much rationality and logic at your disposal. They will surely be the same way about you in times of need.

How do you prevent disputes and ongoing issues from becoming zombies and inflicting pain on you? It's easy - just accept disagreement. Be aware of when you're at a point of no return and are facing an obstruction, and then be able to agree to disagree on the matter.

It's difficult to make a decision when there are potentially huge stakes on the line There aren't any issues that you can reach an agreement on. However, we're all aware that the majority of problems boil down to opinions and disagreements.

In more common usage, it's referred to as a method of communication known as active listening. When executed correctly, it can cause people to talk with you in ways that they didn't think possible... since they've not tried it them.

When you engage in active listening with your lady and prepare yourself to gain deep insight into the reasons she behaves the way she does, and also who she really is on the deepest levels. Understanding your partner is crucial for connecting on a personal level, and strengthening the relationship into a partner in contrast to a surface-level relationship.

How can we learn to engage in active listening so that we can get your woman to be open to you as she would nobody else? Simply focus on these phrases:

You appear to be feeling...

It's as...

What I'm hearing...

So, you're...

Then... (repeat repeating the final few words they used to say)

This is the reason...

It's quite fascinating to observe, how the act of rephrasing someone's words or formulating assumptions based upon the things they've said will always make people elaborate on their point of view and explain it at a deeper level to clarify their thinking.

If you follow the process for long enough and make the right inquiries You could discover the root of someone's worries or intentions. Who wouldn't want an intimate bond with their partner?

Adjust your conflict styles.

If you've read any of Gary Chapman's theories of the five languages of love, then you'll be aware of the specific ways we all display and process emotion.

We may express our love towards our loved ones via one method, however they could express affection through another, so there's a lack of communication and mismatch between love languages.

It's not an issue, since the majority of couples can figure out their preferences in the early stages but it could be the final blow for couples that don't have a good relationship at all.

Similar to how people have different ways of receiving and showing affection, everyone has distinct styles of dealing with conflict. Also, different people react to conflicts and disagreements differently It is therefore important to know your lady's style and then figure out how best to deal with the different styles.

The most popular types of conflict are: co-operating with, competing, accommodating making compromises, and staying clear of. It shouldn't be a surprise to learn that women be in the accommodating and avoidance camps. Men are more likely to have different conflicts and rarely fit into either of the two camps, however, they may be considered to be more explicit in comparison to women.

I believe that the most effective method to deal with criticism or criticizing something that your girlfriend really loves... is to concentrate on your own needs.

Confused? Continue reading.

Instead of making fun of the person's interests and interests be aware of the ways these make you feel disregarded and a slack priority and unimportant. There's nothing necessarily negative about social media however, when they begin to influence the way you see your relationship progressing the issue becomes a justifiable issue and a topic for conversation.

If you are focused on the hobby or interest it becomes a matter of the loss of something that she enjoys. It's a subtle yet distinct distinction in how she'll respond to your approach. If you concentrate on your emotions and not on the action itself and force her to reach her conclusion that she has to alter her behavior to suit your feelings and make you feeling happier.

This can have the unique result of making her want to achieve the initial purpose you were aiming for since it's an affirmative step for her , rather than the reduction in her needs.

They are mental gymnastics at their finest and it is important to think about the effects of the act instead of criticizing the act itself.

Chapter 18: Read Through Women's Profiles

Looking through profiles is fascinating, but for a new guy it can be a bit depressing. A few aspects of "demands" women put on their profiles could make men feel like woman who is a slob!

There are a few demands women must meet include: Must be clever and intelligent and must be strong. should be taller, have a large penis, must be successful economically, should be wealthy and have a great vehicle, must be a successful professional and must have a home and be prepared to marry, must love cats, love dogs and must be a lover of children and be able to amuse me, should love cooking, must enjoy "Game of Thrones" and must enjoy spending time at the sea, take long walks, be able to debate politics, and many more!

One thing that irritates me most is the "Sexual Identities": pansexual and omnisexual. They also include gynosexual, devisexual, sapiosexual autosexual, objectumsexual, androgynosexual, androsexual or graysexual. Find them if you are interested in knowing the meanings behind each. I'll give you one of the more popular ones I've encounter often. It's "Sapiosexual" which is simply that she is influenced by intelligence.

Then I've noticed a lot of women who have these various "Sexual identities" on their profiles. I thought it was important to let you know about this since all of this nonsense can leave an average man depressed. Guys, please don't feel disillusioned when you see an account filled with endless demands. Women will do this in the hope of shaking off the weak guys. I've been with women with an extensive list of demands . I'm pretty sure that I was not even close to fulfilling all of the demands, but I didn't allow that to keep me from sending them a message. However, the majority ended up being excellent women and we end in a wonderful relationship and even developing great relationships. I've met women who said, "Must like to discuss politics" But you know what? We never talked about politics! The conversation was never discussed. Personally, I'm not a fan of the subject of politics. I'm aware that some people who aren't comfortable with someone other's political views. I'm the only one with my own beliefs and every person has the right the right to choose their personal beliefs.

A few times I was on an "one night date" with a lady who's profile read, "I am a tall woman and my husband must be XX inches tall or have a bigger size penis" I was two inches shorter than her minimum requirement for size of her penis. I recall her asking me if I had looked at her profile, and I said yes. Then she askedme "So are you tall?" I said, "Yes I wouldn't have had the courage to message you if I was not. She then said, "Well some men say they're large, but actually aren't. What's the size of your penis?", I message her back with my "pretend" size for the penis, and she responded, "Oh my! Here's my 555-555-5555 number". We were scheduled to meet later that evening, however due to the time constraints we were unable to meet in time. However, the following evening, and she was kind enough to invite me over to her home. I won't go into detail regarding what transpired but she was extremely happy and did not mention anything about my size of penis. In fact I had to take it to her for a while times.

Below is a screenshot of an exchange I had with an individual (her messages are in the yellow boxes) who wrote on her profile "Men Please be at least 6 feet. tall If you're considering communicating with me." Notice that I don't make a huge fuss about her height whenever she mentions it, instead, I just say something humorous and let it be. If you're a man and messaging someone who is larger than you, don't discuss it or say any aspect of it, unless she mentions it Then you can respond by jokingly as I did, and leave it in that manner. It's best to behave as if you've been with taller women in the past and it's not a big deal for you. I've had the pleasure of dating a lot of tall women and I'm able to get the game to win my favor. I enjoy tall women with their long, sexy legs typically in the range of 5'7" and 6'. But, it's not an issue for me, it's just an opinion.

Additionally, some women have written on their profiles "Please don't leave me a message of just a few words or you will not receive an answer." What do I do! I contact them using one of my messages and , yes, I respond! Don't be swayed by the details of what women have written in her personal profile. If she's attractive enough to you , then act and contact her!

Women's Profile Photos

When looking through photos of women make sure that at least two of them are fully-body and close-ups of her face, without filters, and the other of her smiling, with her teeth visible. Be sure that the photos don't go back more than six months or the time you're comfortable with. The majority of times, they'll caption the photo with dates. If they have "Athletic body Type" listed on her profile, make sure that she has pictures to prove it. There are some women who say that they possess an "Athletic body" however are in reality a normal body type, with a large fat booty. In the opposite Some women tick off "Average body type" however are physically fit when they are seen in real life! (Keep that in mind while you're going through your screening process. It's essential to have full body photos.) It's likely that they aren't sure about being healthy, and may be having a low self-esteem. There will also be women who use stupid filters, such as doggy ears, bunny ears and so on. on their images and, when I notice the filters, I go towards the woman next. I'm not in a position to make a request for the woman for a real image of her. If you observe that all of her photos are taken from an upward angle (her looking upwards at the camera) almost all the time, she's an overweight woman. There are also women who tend to be "bottom-heavy" (big hips as well as large legs) and will snap photos of their upper torso and only give the impression that they are an "Athletic body Type". But, there are many men who prefer big hips and large legs, but it's better to see photos and be aware of them before wasting your time and energy.

Younger Women

If I'm referring to young women, I'm speaking of women who are between 21-30. The majority of women within this age range tend to be more irritable in their messaging and tend to lose interest quite quickly. Additionally, having a good Instagram and Snapchat is an advantage (although it is not required). A majority of women in this are active on social media, and, therefore, when you can access their social networks, so you can keep in touch in this manner. It is best to use the "Cocky funny" method (David DeAngelo's "Double your Dating"). If you are messaging them, remember that this process is faster than older women. If you wait too long to send them messages back , they'll lose interest and will continue to pay attention to the other guys who are messaging her.

If you message her, if she's responding immediately, you have the option of waiting at least a minute or two, then send a message back. If she takes more than an hour to respond to your message, it could take from 40 minutes and an hour for reply and if it takes her the whole day to respond you will be able to reply within the same amount of time. the reason I'm not recommending you to wait for a whole day to reply is due to the fact that women receive many men who are who are messaging them. They can get bored or forget you quickly. The messaging method can be utilized by any age class.

Women past their prime
I've noticed that single women in their late thirties to their early forties, who aren't engaged or married to get married, are under pressure from "society" or even friends or family members get their relationships organized by the time they enter their early 30's. It causes them to attempt and get into a relationship, and pressure her partner to join her in a hurry, but not taking the time to establish a relationship. It's not the case that all women in this age range are like this , but a majority of women are. If you're not looking for an intimate relationship or being pressured to sign a contract, I suggest that you take a

break once you begin to notice warning signs. Women may have an affair with you with the intent of keeping you around hoping that you will eventually be committed.

Men, do your best to be sincere about what kind of relationship you're seeking or at the very least offer them some clues as to what you're looking to avoid confusion with these types of women. Make sure to wear condoms when you're engaged sexually with those kinds of women. Actually, with any female (You must always be safe in your sexual interactions, especially in the case of being sexually active with several women on these dating sites or apps. Trust me when I say that most women on these sites are having sexual relations with multiple partners too. It's better to guard yourself (just my opinion). When they know you're not going to commita crime, some are likely to try to become pregnant with you, particularly when you're a handsome man who has your life in good order. Beware of this there is no reason for a child to be living in a home that is broken. Don't let children in wedlock. It can save many problems.

Men often think about themselves when they see the red flags, but when they come from the trance they were in, it's too late. She's "knocked out".

Chapter 19: How To Keep Her Attracted To You, Or How To Have A Long-Term Relationship

Evidently, no one has accomplished this feat for me as of yet. The exception is Darrin. I was a fan of him since kindergarten until the fifth grade, when I realized he was not mature enough. It was the longest I've been in love with anyone. My longest love affair is with my dog. Seventeen years. May she rest in peace.

However, if the man I'd like had adhered to my two principal rules it would have been different. It seems I'm only interested in the scumbags. We'll talk about that later.

Treat her as human beings and revert to her behavior when she tells you to. This means always. Let's look at what the guys have to say and the reason why it's likely to be manipulative"bullshit.

Okay, I'm actually in agreement with each and every one of the headings I saw on the initial list I searched. I'll share the headline, then I'll give you my own perspective from an individual woman's view.

Respect her when you're with her.

In the beginning, I'll alter the title. Always be respectful. This is a reference to the kindness aspect. Don't discuss her with your friends. If you have your disagreements and fights only between the two of you then your family and friends will not have an opinion that is biased of the person you love the most. We always overlook telling them when the SO apologized.

It advises you to open doors, remove chairs, hand her your jacket in case she's cold, and all the stuff. I'll add it to the above. If she opens the door to you, walk straight through it. If she is willing to pay, simply acknowledge her thanks.

It suggests that you pick your clothes with greater care and maintain proper hygiene. Heck, yes!

Avoid all offensive behavior in public, such as swearing or spouting. Ok, I'm not the person to tell that you shouldn't swear. Also, don't be a snorer or even belching, for that matter. However, do make sure you edit yourself when you are in public for both of your accounts. Do I really have to include the sound of a dog's flinch? Yes, I understand how it can happen, however you need create it as the non-silent but deadly kind with the blame on your dog. However, she'll recognize it after some time. If you're forced to make a noise in public, try to make it fun. When I was subscribing I dropped a quiet one as I passed by the popular teenager. I thought, "Duuude!" I do not know if he was still popular the following day. I was only being a sub. It wasn't my issue.

*I love your smile. It's adorable. It makes me smile.

I love the way your eyes sparkle when you speak about...

I love the feeling that I feel when I see that you feel like everything will be alright.

*I am awed by the teamwork we can achieve when we are doing this...

I love coming home to you.
I love waking up to you.
I love your scent.
*I love you greater than my dog.
You're very skilled with...
*You're very smart in...

Let Her Know That She is in Your Head

There's no need to message her throughout the day long, and you don't have to reply immediately. If she's a mature adult, she'll know that you're not in the mood. She's busy too. You should be texting her at minimum every day, with more than "Sup?" Ask a specific inquiry about her day, or even send an inside joke or write, "Hey, just thinking about your day. We hope you have a wonderful today." It's it adorable, and if it's not all day you're an adult with work and a social life. However, if it's just an hour or so it's still a significant aspect of your life.

Surprise Her by presenting her with Romantic Gestures

Yes. Do this. The article I found suggested a playlist of songs that bring back memories of her. Yes. You can do that. If you've got "our track," it needs to be the first. Don't add Stupid Girl or You're a Bitch or any other rap song about sloppy ass hoes. You're welcome.

The article also suggests slipping notes of love into her locker. It's okay, we're talking about the long-term here, folks. "M" is the word. or, at a minimum The F word. It's it's not it's the Fuck word. It is available everywhere. It's the Future word. High schoolers are aware of whom they'd like to be married to, yet they've no idea of how to file their taxes. They'll have to.

Love notes are an excellent idea, however when you're in high school concentrate on your academics and be a good child. You can just throw them in the console of her car one day. Put some in your hoodie pocket. The hoodie will be borrowing, without returning.

Request to borrow her car one day. Return it clean and with an entire tank of gas and twelve roses placed on her seat. The girl will be raving about it for months.

Consider these preventive measures instead of fixing. It's a lot simpler to do this.

The list suggests getting her something that she can wear everyday to show her how you love her. Okay, no. Did this article be written by a male? Men aren't aware of what to do when shopping for female clothing. They don't know how choose their clothes. We're perfectly capable of picking our own clothes Thanks.

I'll provide a few ideas of actual ones. Love notepads and the playlists are great. My car wash concept is great. Here's some additional.

Take note of what's in the fridge. Take her food items according to her preferences occasionally.

*Send her a novel about her favorite celebrity.

* Randomly deposit money into her PayPal.

Buy her gifts for Christmas from Amazon. Everyone likes surprise presents! Items she'd love, perhaps lotion or body spray baskets, movies she's not yet bought or similar to those hanging in her home.

• Plan a picnic in a place that is different - the mountains a rooftop, or the bed of the truck.

Have Fun and make her laugh

Everyone loves to laugh. Make sure to include plenty of laughter in your relationship. Don't be upset in the event that you go into a conversation and she takes the topic up.

However, be careful not to play with her when she isn't happy with it. Be sure that you're not mocking the woman for doing something which is hurtful. If she asks you to take a step back, follow through.

Two rules that are fundamental be treated as if you would treat a human and be quiet when she asks to- they're more than just about sexual sex. They're applicable to all situations. If she claims she's not willing to talk about it, just try to believe her rather than forcing her to discuss it even if she's not happy and her words don't appear right. Refrain from talking about it.

The beginning of the end or the end of the Beginning

If she's good as well, and duped you're totally free to cheat, aren't you? No? So why are so many men doing it?

Keep her in your heart and love. It's not because you wish for her to be cheating even though you shouldn't and you are in love with her. In that regard it's not your spouse's responsibility to stop any cheater from happening or cheating, and it's not the spouse's fault if they cheat. If you're old enough to marry or live in a home together and live together, then you're big enough to be able to hold your pants on and be a good person.

Remember to keep the love notes as well as the gifts that surprise you and date nights, especially if you have kids. Keep those love notes you left each to each other. Look them over after an epic battle to remind yourself of the person you were when you were married, before things became a hindrance. If you continue to do these, it's not the same 10 notes that you've been doing after each fight. It's only going to take two or three fights.

Don't believe a lot of the good-hearted but not really poor marriage advice you've received.

As in "never be angry at bedtime." This is nonsense. You can sleep in a state of anger. Avoid doing it, obviously. What's more likely is you are trying to follow the rulesone of the following scenarios: a: you settle your problems, but it's not the same battle that you fight all the time or b) you're fighting the same thing and you're up all night at night, feeling more tired and angry, making things that you regret in the morning and by the time the day arrives, you're upset by what they did to be sorry for what you did? That's the way I felt. Don't go to sleep and be angry. It's okay. You can go to sleep. You'll be able to see it clearly when you wake up.

Also known as "marriage can be 50/50." The marriage isn't 50/50. A perfect union is one that's 100/100. Each of you is providing 100% of what you've got. This will depend depending on the individual, and on the day. I'm afflicted by five chronic ailments. I'm not able do what people are able to accomplish. If I was to marry I'd like him to be an exceptional man who could acknowledge that, and not simply think I'm lazy.

Don't fall for the "men aren't able to express their feelings" rubbish. If you're able communicate with her when you're upset You don't need be waiting until you're mad and then get into a screaming contest.

As Semisonic states, "Every new beginning comes from the end of a previous beginning."

Chapter 20: What Makes A Perfect Date Work So Well

What will she feel: a series of emotions becoming more intense.

What can I do to create these strong emotions?

A lot of people think that the key difference between a date that has an enjoyable end and one that has a bad end is in the topic of conversations.

With an excellent display ability and a broad range of topics that are interesting it is possible to get her to try various emotions, including intense ones. To be successful, you must be a proficient speaker, enthusiastic and knowledgeable about how to communicate to others emotions during a discussion.

This reminds me of a chief scouts who share an engaging story to children or an older man who tells stories of terror to kids at Halloween. Well, the story as it is stated and the breaks, the tension is there all the time the content doesn't matter. The truth is that a story of horror will not scare anyone if it is poorly presented.

If you're a professional with good presentation abilities, make use of them and make the most of your strengths.

But the purpose of this guide is to make the things simpler.

Anyone can impress a woman during the first meeting, even you're indifferent and aloof.

I'll offer some examples. Let's flip the situation upside down and take pleasure in putting yourself in the shoes of. Let's suppose that she's asking you to take a trip to organize the information. 2 different girls, 2 different dates. Imagine a variety of situations.

The first girl takes you to a macrobiotic/vegetarian restaurant. On your second night, you travel together to different shoe stores. The third time she invites you to enjoy a cup of coffee with her and her friends. You might not want to accept, but you decide to accept. The fourth time the woman asks for you to accompany her to a shop outside of in the town ... WOW.

The girl in the second invites you to play of soccer, in which you're the only male, and the girls are playing in a topless. After the game is finished then you head to the barbecue at the beach. The players who lost are required to pay for the drink of the other team. The guests are welcoming and organized In the case of the weather there are a variety of tents available , and those who want could stay to sleep on the beach by the bonfire. You will be amazed to discover that this girl can teach you how to surf, and the next morning , a private surfing lesson awaits you.

Have you ever tried to live in the present moment? What feelings did you experience? Did you enjoy them? Have you noticed the differences in the girl's first date and her second?

Now, you realize that I haven't talked about discussions on TOPICS. The emotions you've felt are primarily due to activities and places. The actions you have performed as well as the locations where you go on a date will be the reason why the woman feel intensely emotional. Note this sentence.

Don't worry, I'll draw it out for you, and then you can read it again.

You're now the one who takes the woman out. Picture the situation.

First date:

You're dressed in a chic way you head out and find her to the home and she's late. Take her to a chic eatery that's a little outside town eating well, and talking all night, and then drive your daughter back home.

Second date:

You dress in a classy manner when you leave and take her at the front of the house, and then go to the movie to see a play and then have ice cream and then take her to home.

Third date:

You get her from the front door of your home Go to a bar and try to bring her to your home, but you're not able to, you receive an unintentional kiss, but perhaps it was just a cheeky gesture.

Fourth date:

You take her from her home, she's late, you take her to a lovely eatery in the city before taking her to your home, where you go to chat about nothing for one hour, and then you kiss her.

Fifth date:

You ran into a few issues getting it all organized and she wasn't always responsive when you sent messages. You dress up as a cool girl, and you take her to her home to dance with your friends. After the night has ended, you could make her return home to you. Then you kiss her. start to dress her then she says it's too late and you bring her to home.

This is the best!

The classic date sequence. What's wrong? What emotion did you cause her feel?

I'm telling you: nothing is new.

What do you think if your first date was similar to this?

Are you aware of the initial love story in the film Hitch? The actor took the girl on a water-scooter, and later to a museum located on an island. Different emotions, same date. You are the one who determines the sequence of emotions that allow them to try, and then plan the steps for the event. To increase the connection to strengthen the bond between your, length of time you spend together isn't important it's all about quality.

It is a way to make her experience so many different experiences in one go. You will let her experience the same feelings you've experienced for years. This will build a strong relationship between you. You will share unforgettable moments, and she will be able to remember the times she spent with you.

The bond you share with someone who is not in your life right now is the mixture of emotions that arise from the memories of times that were spent together.

They usually develop after a series of dates. In certain instances, 91% of guys take her four times a day at the eatery (this amounts to just one emotion or tiny bit more). The date you plan will undoubtedly be unique special, memorable, and memorable. It will not be anything like the kind of events she was confronted with in recent times.

I'm certain that you'll begin to think about the ways in which you can make the Perfect Date is effectively POWERFUL.

Release the handbrake and settle down. You aren't fully prepared yet, and there is still a lot to master.
Let's continue.

Conclusion

I hope that this book has helped you understand the subject of dating. There are a lot of things to consider when you are dating, and I'm hoping you learn something useful from this book. Being a single individual is not without sacrifices, yet it also offers many rewards such as being self-sufficient and prioritizing your needs.

But it is true that having a relationship with someone else and creating it from scratch isn't an issue either. It's actually a fantastic feeling, and one which should be enjoyed by anyone when the time is right. If you're looking to meet someone don't be afraid to make yourself available. There's no harm in looking for love and seeing what the world can offer you. Be sure to choose the "right" person to share your good and sad ones with.

In The book, finding that perfect love interest isn't an simple task, and it nearly always takes a lot of effort due to a variety of reasons. The scenarios in the book could occur in your own relationship, but it's always good to be prepared if you are in a situation. Be sure to remember to follow the suggestions and guidelines I provided because, it is likely that you will encounter a number of instances that are very similar to or even closely similar to the situations I've discussed within the text.

Always be sure to draw attention towards the ideal person as everything that is good will come along. Be honest and don't be afraid to let go of the person you are thinking that they aren't the ideal partner. Don't force a date since if you do, the next stage of your relationship could be made to happen. It is not something you want to happen. to happen to you. This can cause your life to be more miserable and stressful in comparison to the life you had before you began dating. This defeats the purpose of dating, so make sure to bring things into an overall perspective.

No matter what the circumstance regardless of whether you have failed in relationship once or several times It is crucial to be convinced there is a "right" one for you is within the next few months. Don't lose hope or be discouraged because once you've done that you will find that everything else that you do will be negative. Your aim is to be content and regardless of whether dating is the right choice for you, you must give yourself the chance to try it. You owe it to yourself, so don't ever let yourself down.

There are not all dates that are perfect and perfect, even though you follow each and every aspect of this book. Don't blame yourself when things don't work out. It is known as fate and it's always right. It is a feeling you can feel as well and take your time waiting for it.

www.ingramcontent.com/pod-product-compliance
Lightning Source LLC
Chambersburg PA
CBHW071836080526
44589CB00012B/1018